No More Open Doors

Mission: To Proclaim Transformation and Truth
Publisher: Transformed Publishing, Cocoa, FL
Website: www.transformedpublishing.com
Email: transformedpublishing@gmail.com

ISBN: 978-1-953241-60-3 (paperback)

ISBN: 978-1-953241-61-0 (Ebook)

**Pastor
Kimani Smith**

NO
MORE
OPEN
DOORS

Dedication

To my beloved wife, Datnee Smith, whose unwavering encouragement, prayers, and guidance have consistently led my heart toward seeking the King. Your steadfast support has been my anchor throughout this journey.

My profound gratitude extends to my four remarkable children—Nehemiah, Kimberlee, Daniel, and Naomi—who bestowed upon me the precious gift of fatherhood. Your inspiration continually propels me to strive for greater goodness and growth.

I am indebted to my parents, Pastor Mullery Jean Pierre, and Cacheta Jean Pierre. Your ceaseless prayers and spiritual battles on my behalf have shaped my path, allowing me to stand where I am today.

To my dear siblings—Fatima, Mark, Monique, Jasmine, Elijah, Rose, and Jennifer—thank you for your unwavering belief in my vision. Your unwavering support and encouragement propelled me to complete this book.

God's Kingdom Church Florida, where I serve as lead Pastor, holds a special place in my heart. The experiences within its walls have molded me in ways beyond imagination. To our pastoral staff—Pastor Alberto, Pastor Veronica, and Pastor Nancy—your continued support in ministry has been invaluable. Your words of encouragement fueled my determination to finish writing this book.

Last but not least, I dedicate this work to Luigi Cozzolino and Amin Said—my true friends who never hesitate to challenge me. Your unwavering commitment to seeking God, standing up for righteousness, and never giving up inspires me daily.

May this book carry the essence of these dedications—a testament to love, faith, and unwavering support.

Table of Contents

Preface

This book was not written to drum up the spirit of fear. Fear does not come from God but from the enemy. Neither was this book written to portray Satan and his demonic kingdom as all-powerful. While he is a powerful foe, our God is greater and has defeated him already on the cross. As it is written in Colossians 2:15, "And having disarmed the powers and authorities, he made a public spectacle of them, triumphing over them by the cross."

No More Open Doors, was written to be a Biblical resource so you are better able to war against the enemy. I have lost time, energy, and relationships trying to fight spiritual battles the wrong way.

This book proclaims the supremacy of Christ over all principalities (army of Satan) and provides you with a strategic understanding of how the enemy invades our lives. My favorite part is that we have been given complete authority, through Jesus Christ, to command the enemy to leave us and all that belongs to us.

May God bless you as you trade in your shoes for combat boots. Let's go to war!

We have assurance that one of Jesus' primary missions was to defeat, disarm, and humiliate the enemy. All of this was accomplished on the cross.

Keep Colossians 2:15 at the forefront of your mind. Know Satan has been defeated. He has been disarmed. His weapons have been removed from him. He has been humiliated and made a public spectacle.

We do not fight a war unaware of the outcome. We fight from the place of victory. Jesus Christ's victory has become our victory, and we fight from what has already been accomplished through Jesus Christ.

Introduction
Deliverance: The Children's Bread

I came into the Ministry of Deliverance by simply praying, "Lord, You casted out demons in the Bible and I want to cast them out as well."

When I prayed this prayer, God was faithful to teach me how to pray for others to be set free. During this process, I wrestled with a lot of questions. Questions such as:

❖ Can a Christian have a demon?

❖ How can a Christian be demonized?

❖ What are the theological reasons I can reference, to be foundationally grounded in the Ministry of Deliverance?

Through much study, research, and prayer, God gave me a theological framework for His Ministry of Deliverance. Before reading the many examples of those who have been set free, you must also understand this theological framework. What I am about to share is a culmination of many pastors, teachers, and books I have researched on deliverance; the results of my own search through the Scriptures; and what God has revealed to me personally.

Let's read some Biblical accounts of demonization and deliverance.

Jesus left that place and went to the vicinity of Tyre. He entered a house and did not want anyone to know it; yet he could not keep his presence secret. In fact, as soon as she heard about him, a woman whose little daughter was possessed by an impure spirit came and fell at his feet. The woman was a Greek, born in Syrian Phoenicia. She begged Jesus to drive the demon out of her daughter.

"First let the children eat all they want," he told her, "for it is not right to take the children's bread and toss it to the dogs."

"Lord," she replied, "even the dogs under the table eat the children's crumbs."

Then he told her, "For such a reply, you may go; the demon has left your daughter."

She went home and found her child lying on the bed, and the demon gone.

-Mark 7:24–30

This story, more than any other story, speaks so much to the Ministry of Deliverance. It provides clarity and demonstrates the priority Jesus placed on who should receive the Ministry of Deliverance.

A Canaanite woman cried out to Jesus for help. She begged Jesus to drive the demon out of her daughter, who was experiencing spiritual torment. In fact, the Scripture explicitly states, "My daughter is demon-possessed and suffering terribly."

> A Canaanite woman from that vicinity came to him, crying out, "Lord, Son of David, have mercy on me! My daughter is demon-possessed and suffering terribly."

-Matthew 15:22

The term demon-possessed, triggers many thoughts in the mind of a Christian, such as, *Can demons take ownership of people?* Know this, the devil does not own anything.

> "Behold, all souls are Mine; the soul of the father as well as the soul of the son is Mine; the soul who sins shall die.["]

-Ezekiel 18:4 NKJV

All souls belong to the Lord. Satan does not own anyone, especially *not* a believer. Let me say this right from the start, a Christian cannot be possessed by a demon. A Christian can be oppressed but not possessed. The reason why this concept has resulted in so much confusion is because the word translated 'possessed' in Scripture is not a correct interpretation in comparison to the Greek.

The word is actually 'Daimonizomai'[1] (dahee-moni-d-zoma-hee) It means to be demonized; to be under the influence of a demon.

The word 'influence' is very important because it sets the tone for deliverance ministry, which helps people break free in areas of their lives where the enemy has had influence. Influence does not mean possession. For example, if someone smokes weed or takes a pill, it would *not* be said that they are possessed by a drug, but rather they are under the influence of that substance.

The Biblical woman referenced in this story asked Jesus to help her daughter who was demonized under the influence of the enemy.

The disciples told Jesus to send her away, but Jesus answered, "I was sent only to the lost sheep of Israel" (*see* Matthew 15:24).

Jesus affirmed His mission to the lost people of Israel. He told her His priority is the covenantal people of God. The woman was full of despair and begged Jesus to help her. Jesus said something we must pay attention to, "It is not right to take the children's bread and toss it to the dogs" (*see* Matthew 15:26).

What is the children's bread in the context of this passage? The children's bread is deliverance. Jesus told her it is the children of God, the believers, who have the right to it. He asserted that deliverance belongs to God's children first. As His children, we have the right to be free from lying, pornography, lust, rejection, depression, loneliness, sadness, and every other tormenting corrupt entity.

What is the basis for this right? Being a child of God. Hence, deliverance belongs to you.

This woman exercised great faith and demonstrated her belief when she called Jesus 'Lord' and rebutted, "even the dogs under the table eat the children's crumbs." Simply stated, she told Jesus, "Lord, I don't need the whole loaf just give me a crumb."

When Jesus saw her faith in Him. He granted her request and gave her the bread she asked for. Jesus delivered her daughter from demonic torment.

Notice, in this occurrence, it was her faith in Jesus that granted her the right to deliverance. In other words, her faith in Him made the woman His daughter and therefore a recipient of the right to have deliverance-*the children's bread.*

Therefore, deliverance is *not* a ministry for the unsaved but for those who have placed their faith in Jesus.

Another story in the Bible which illustrates this point is when Jesus healed a crippled woman on the Sabbath.

On a Sabbath Jesus was teaching in one of the synagogues, and a woman was there who had been crippled by a spirit for eighteen years. She was bent over and could not straighten up at all. When Jesus saw her, he called her forward and said to her, "Woman, you are set free from your infirmity." Then he put his hands on her, and immediately she straightened up and praised God.

Indignant because Jesus had healed on the Sabbath, the synagogue leader said to the people, "There are six days for work. So come and be healed on those days, not on the Sabbath."

The Lord answered him, "You hypocrites! Doesn't each of you on the Sabbath untie your ox or donkey from the stall and lead it out to give it water? Then should not this woman, a daughter of Abraham, whom Satan has kept bound for eighteen long years, be set free on the Sabbath day from what bound her?"

When he said this, all his opponents were humiliated, but the people were delighted with all the wonderful things he was doing.

-Luke 13:10–17

Jesus taught in the Jewish synagogue, in their place of worship, their church. There, He encounters a woman who was crippled by a spirit of infirmity, bound by Satan for eighteen years.

Notice, this woman was in the place of worship, to worship God, in church and experiencing prolonged sickness. The root of her sickness was *not* biological. This sickness manifested through an unclean spirit of infirmity. A demon influenced her health and caused her to be crippled.

Jesus called her forward, identified the root cause of her sickness, and declared, "'Woman, you are set free from your infirmity.' Then he put his hands on her, and immediately she straightened up and praised God" (*see* Luke 13:12-13).

This Scriptural account proves all sickness is *not* biological. Some sicknesses are the result of demonic oppression influencing the lives of people. Once the spirit that caused the disease has been dealt with the physical body heals. It is *not* uncommon. When someone receives deliverance, the sickness caused by that spirit leaves.

When Jesus executed this woman's right of deliverance, the leaders of the synagogue were indignant because Jesus healed on the Sabbath day. Jesus was also upset at the church leaders. Let's review this text one more time.

Indignant because Jesus had healed on the Sabbath, the synagogue leader said to the people, "There are six days for work. So come and be healed on those days, not on the Sabbath."

The Lord answered him, "You hypocrites! Doesn't each of you on the Sabbath untie your ox or donkey from the stall and lead it out to give it water? Then should not this woman, a daughter of Abraham, whom Satan has kept bound for eighteen long years, be set free on the Sabbath day from what bound her?"

-Luke 13:14–16

Jesus was upset because these religious leaders would untie their animals and lead them to get water on the Sabbath but would not let a child of God receive deliverance.

By referring to the woman as a daughter of Abraham, He is emphasizing she is part of the covenantal people of God. He called her daughter, a child of God, who has the right to deliverance. She is more important than an animal needing water. She is a child of God and has the right to be set free from the influence of Satan.

In one breath Jesus said something we don't want to miss, "this woman, a daughter of Abraham, whom

Satan has kept bound for eighteen long years." Pay attention to the fact there is no objection from the religious leaders that this is a child of God who is bound. The only objection was that Jesus chose to heal on the Sabbath. They more so saw what Jesus did as a violation of the Sabbath, the day deemed by God to *not* work, but to rest and keep holy. Jesus did not break the Sabbath by healing this woman. In fact, He gave this woman rest from her infirmity.

When Jesus healed her and pointed out the hypocrisy of the leaders who denied deliverance of a believer but cared for animals on the Sabbath, they were humiliated, however the people rejoiced.

There are many misconceptions about Christians being oppressed. People think that if a Christian is battling oppression, they are not saved. But this is surely not the case. Apostle Paul, a great Biblical Christian suffered oppression. As we read a portion of his story, we get a glimpse through a window into the nature of oppression, and how it takes place in the life of a believer.

> [O]r because of these surpassingly great revelations. Therefore, in order to keep me from becoming conceited, I was given a thorn in my flesh, a messenger of Satan, to torment me. Three times I pleaded with the Lord to take it away from me. But he said to me, "My

grace is sufficient for you, for my power is made perfect in weakness." Therefore I will boast all the more gladly about my weaknesses, so that Christ's power may rest on me.

-2 Corinthians 12:7–9

Apostle Paul was blessed to receive a revelation of heaven. He was taken into the third heaven and heard things he could not repeat (*see* 2 Corinthians 12:1-4). To keep him humble, God allowed oppression in Paul's life. Paul referred to it as *a thorn in the flesh*. Most people familiar with this text, have accepted the fact that Paul had an issue in the flesh, but do not readily accept the origin of this thorn because it does not sit well with the traditional perception of theology. Instead, it is glossed over and pretended like what Paul said does not exist. Paul's statement was bold, "a messenger of Satan."

The Greek word is 'angelos'[2] which means messenger or angel.

> ángelos [messenger, angel], archángelos [archangel], isángelos [like an angel]

Paul is a believer who was tormented in His flesh by a messenger of Satan. Some scholars believe he might have said this because he may have had poor eyesight. We do not know what the thorn was, but we know for sure that it tormented him in his flesh and was of a demonic source. It came from Satan. *Where was the torment?* In the flesh.

Christians cannot be demonized in their regenerated spirit, the place where the Holy Spirit has sealed them (*see* Ephesians 1:13 and Ephesians 4:30). They can be oppressed in their flesh. The oppression believers face is in their flesh. Paul recognized he was tormented, by a thorn in the flesh, from Satan.

The Ministry of Deliverance breaks the influence of the enemy in the flesh, the place targeted by demonic agents, in the lives of believers.

How does a Christian open a door to oppression? Demonic spirits cannot just enter a Christian's life. The spiritual realm works on legalities. The enemy needs a legal right to be able to access a believer.

Three ways a Christian can give legal right to the enemy to enter their life are willful sin, ignorance, and generational curses. I will briefly introduce these points of entry and will elaborate more as we continue our journey through *No More Open Doors*.

- Willful Sin

   "In your anger do not sin": Do not let the sun go down while you are still angry, and do not give the devil a foothold.

   -Ephesians 4:26–27

The Bible says, "do not give the devil a foothold." The Greek uses the word, 'tópos'.

tópos[3] [place]
A. Greek Literature.
1. Simple Use. In common usage this word means
    a. "territory," "land," "area," "locality,"
    b. "district," "town," "dwelling place," and
    c. "place"

The Word of God cautions us to *not* yield any area, territory, or place to the enemy.

Throughout this book, I will share real life experiences from those who opened the doorway of demonization through willful sin. Willful sin implies a person knows what they are doing is wrong, and they do it anyway, violating the word of God. These choices have spiritual consequences that go far beyond the momentary pleasure of sin and result in oppression.

- <u>Ignorance</u>

Many people unknowingly open the door to evil activity. I have had many prayer sessions with people who have participated in occult practices without understanding the dangers of them. Satan does a good job hiding in plain sight.

Some of these ignorant acts can be as simple as putting on demonic Santeria beads. Just wearing them alone invites ungodly spirits into one's life. I know a person who watched a witchcraft ceremony but didn't participate in it. Just the mere watching out of curiosity was enough to cause them to be bound.

[M]y people are destroyed from lack of knowledge. "Because you have rejected knowledge, I also reject you as my priests; because you have ignored the law of your God, I also will ignore your children.

-Hosea 4:6

▪   Generational Curses

Legal ground to oppress a believer can be established through generational curses. These are spiritual doors *not* opened by the person themselves, but by their parents or someone further back in the bloodline.

And he passed in front of Moses, proclaiming, "The Lord, the Lord, the compassionate and gracious God, slow to anger, abounding in love and faithfulness, maintaining love to thousands, and forgiving wickedness, rebellion and sin. Yet he does not leave the guilty unpunished; he punishes the children and their children for the sin of the parents to the third and fourth generation."

Moses bowed to the ground at once and worshiped.

-Exodus 34:6–8

Generational curses open spiritual doors that give Satan access to the bloodline, even to the ones who did *not* initially open the door. My go-to example of this is found in the life of King David, which I share in detail in Chapter 3. God forgave David of his sin but told David through Nathan the prophet, "Now, therefore, the sword will never depart from your house, because you despised me and took the wife of Uriah the Hittite to be your own"" (2 Samuel 12:10).

As we serve God and lead people through the freedom of deliverance, we must have a strong theological framework and foundational confidence that God will liberate the people He brings to us, when we reveal and operate in the principles of deliverance.

It's my hope that this book encourages you and makes you aware of the enemy's tactics, and in turn causes you to walk in freedom.

---

[1]Gerhard Kittel, Gerhard Friedrich, and Geoffrey William Bromiley, Theological Dictionary of the New Testament, Abridged in One Volume (Grand Rapids, MI: W.B. Eerdmans, 1985), 137.
[2]Gerhard Kittel, Gerhard Friedrich, and Geoffrey William Bromiley, Theological Dictionary of the New Testament, Abridged in One Volume (Grand Rapids, MI: W.B. Eerdmans, 1985), 12.
[3]Gerhard Kittel, Gerhard Friedrich, and Geoffrey William Bromiley, Theological Dictionary of the New Testament, Abridged in One Volume (Grand Rapids, MI: W.B. Eerdmans, 1985), 1184.

1: Doorway of the Eyes

"The eye is the lamp of the body. If your eyes are healthy, your whole body will be full of light. But if your eyes are unhealthy, your whole body will be full of darkness. If then the light within you is darkness, how great is that darkness!["]

-Matthew 6:22-23

In this passage of Scripture, the eyes are described as lamps, but *not* just ordinary lamps. Lamps that have the ability to take in light or darkness. Jesus said if your eyes are bad then your whole body is full of darkness. It's easy to miss this. Jesus spoke about the first door, the doorway of the eyes.

The eyes were created to take in images and scenery. Unfortunately, when God designed our eyes, He did not design them with a filter. What they see, they take in, whether good or bad, in its full potency. Jesus said, "But if your eyes are unhealthy, your whole body will be full of darkness." Jesus is not speaking about cataracts or some form of sickness that causes blindness. Our eyes are bad when we let bad things in. When evil is entertained with the eyes, darkness is given access into our lives. When we entertain our eyes with good things that please the Lord, we allow what is good into our lives.

This may sound elementary. Maybe you are thinking, *What's so big about this revelation?* Well, let me tell you my story. One day, I decided to watch a scary movie that was on television, knowing I hate scary movies. I felt the Holy Spirit tell me not to watch the movie. Sadly, I did not listen. After I watched the movie, I started having a hard time reading the Bible and praying. This went on for weeks. As I took the bus home, in the middle of the night, I prayed and asked God what was wrong. The Lord told me it was the movie I watched.

I had opened a door to the enemy, and he was blocking me from the Lord. Once the Lord revealed this to me, I renounced what I did and confessed my sin. I prayed a simple prayer, "I renounce given permission to the enemy by what I watched. God, please forgive me. I offer my eyes to be used for Your glory and Your glory alone."

What was the doorway in which the enemy entered into my life? It was the doorway of the eyes. You cannot counsel someone who is demonized, nor can you give advice to a stronghold. No, it must be torn down. This will be discussed later. The key takeaway is, I became bound because of what I watched. Yes, that spirit was cast out, but the enemy came through the entry point of my eyes.

The television is one of the biggest doorways to demonization. I have watched television shows change over the years, progressively intensifying the promotion of witchcraft and the occult. There are shows about witches and demons that cause us to fantasize about the supernatural. They feed us thoughts of having power outside of the Spirit of God. These are all different forms of demonology. Listen to some of the things these characters say and research the meaning behind the terms such as astral projection and reiki energy healing. These are New Age terms and tap into demonic sources for power. I have learned over the years the tactics of the enemy are cunning. I no longer look at things on the surface but research television shows, movies, and products in order to ensure I am not unknowingly entertaining something that displeases the Lord.

On one occasion, I was praying for someone who we will call Susie. She began to shake, and her hand began to curl. I did not know what to make of it. The Holy Spirit told me, *purge*. I said to the Lord that is exactly what I am doing, *purging*. The Lord said to me again *purge*.

Then I asked the young lady, "Did you watch any horror movies?" She said she watched a particular movie three times. The Lord gave me the revelation - *she was bound by what she had watched*. I led her in prayer to renounce the access given to these spirits by watching the movie. I commanded the spirit to leave, and she was released from the torment. What was interesting is that this young lady did not even know the enemy was there. She had no idea she opened a door to the enemy by what she watched.

One of the biggest tactics of the enemy is to remain hidden in plain sight. Oftentimes people who are bound are completely unaware of what is binding them. *Why is that?* When bound by the enemy, behavior traits, characteristics, and things people have struggled with all their lives seem to be normal. So, they go unchallenged. This is why the Ministry of Deliverance is so important. God will often use a minister of deliverance to expose areas where the enemy has been hiding.

I hate to say this, but there is not much I can sit through and watch on television without feeling like I have sinned against the Holy Spirit. I used to think that because I am an adult, and the television show said eighteen and up or TV-14, it was acceptable to watch. But five minutes into the show, after the first F-bomb, the Holy Spirit would convict me. Even though it may have been a great action movie, what was supposed to bring me pleasure and relaxation brought the feeling of being disconnected from God because I knew He was not pleased by what I chose for entertainment. The reality is things only have two purposes. To bring glory to God or *not* to bring glory to God. We can try to justify our leisure time all we want, but the truth is we are either participating in things that please God or do *not* please Him.

Maybe you're thinking, I am ridiculous, and no one can live their life so carefully, guarding their eyes from evil, besides a little smut won't kill anyone. Well, please look at this list my skeptical friend.

The following is a summarized list of acknowledgements made by widely known serial killers:

- Pictures of past victims and pornographic videos and magazines were viewed before *hunting* new victims (seventeen boys and men).

- Hardcore pornography had a 'crystallizing effect' and was attributed to violent tendencies, rape, and mutilation murder.

- Pornography had a 'devastating effect' ending in the rape and murder of five young boys.

- Pictures of naked women and pornography were noted as the *blame* for the murder of at least fifty-three women and children by one serial killer.

- A library of anatomy books, pornographic magazines, and horror and adventure novels were the obsession of another serial killer.

- It was reported by his wife that this serial killer, credited with killing at least thirty-three young men and boys, had erratic mood swings and a large pornographic magazine collection centered around young boys.

- A serial killer of ten people kept meticulous records of his fantasies and crimes and had an extensive pornography collection.

- A member of a cult, drug user, involved with sadistic and child pornography, and violent crime is known for having killed over a dozen people.

- By being exposed to explicit pictures of a family member raping women and severing the heads of soldiers, in turn, he is noted as killing at least thirteen people himself.

- By using pornography and detective magazines for erotic stimulation, one killed women, then raped them post-mortem.

- Became obsessed with homosexual pornography, began killing at the age of fourteen and is known to have killed one hundred eight people.

- Had a penchant for prostitutes and pornography. Took pornographic pictures of his victims then strangled them to death. Eleven victims are noted.

- Indisputable evidence of internet searches for preteen girl pornography was used to convict this killer.

- Viewed online photographs of young girls and pornographic cartoons depicting rape prior to abducting a victim.

All these serial killers have one thing in common. They opened the door to the enemy by what they watched. Pornography led to murder. Do you see the connection here? Can you piece the puzzle together?

Pornography devalues a person to the point to which they are *not* seen as a real person but *something* to fulfill another person's needs. In a sense, they have been killed off in the heart and now seen as an object and not human.

Devaluing human life precedes murder. You may say, *I am crazy.* Well, let me pose a question, *How are we as a human society able to promote abortion?*

Now, don't get mad at me and throw this book away. Come back, sit down, and take a breather. We must be honest, most of society doesn't call a baby in the womb a baby. They are called a fetus. This term takes away every human characteristic of a baby and allows for the mother and father to kill the child. *Why?* Because *before* the baby was killed, human life was devalued.

The serial killers I researched when preparing this book, did not have the spiritual intelligence to understand *what* they were letting into their lives. They were blind to the devil's schemes. They did not know when they gazed at their first pornographic film that the enemy was giving them more than just sensual pleasure but a doorway to hell itself. Let's pause for a moment to really digest this thing.

When human life is devalued, in any way, it will lead to racism, sex trafficking, prostitution, murder, and death. *What we watch does affect what we do!* The ever-present accessibility of television and internet content has resulted in an oversexualized generation. What we take into our eyes affects what we do. *Why?* Our eyes let in light or darkness. Light in Scripture signifies goodness, good works, Christianity, and even Jesus Christ Himself.

Darkness in Scripture represents sin, evil, and Satan. Let's go back to my story of bondage through the movie I watched. The million-dollar question is, *How did I as a Christian end up in spiritual bondage?* To answer this question, we need to understand the principles of the kingdom. The kingdom of God operates through legalities, *legal ground.* The devil just can't come into a believer's life and trouble them. Let me preempt this point by saying I am not talking about temptation or spiritual resistance as we do the work of the Lord or lead a godly life. I am talking about the devil feeling comfortable enough to make his home in you.

The bondage that transpired through the movie I watched tormented me for weeks. I told you I was unable to read my Bible and pray. *Why?* Because I chose at the time to watch a demonic movie. When I watched the movie, I gave *permission* to the enemy to harass me. Permission is a big word pertaining to deliverance ministry. *Why?* Because oftentimes people are demonized because of a doorway they opened willingly.

In the book of Numbers, chapters 22-24, we read the story of a prophet by the name of Balaam. The king of the Moabites hired him to curse the people of Israel. To literally put a spell on them.

> [So Balak] sent messengers to summon Balaam son of Beor, who was at Pethor, near the Euphrates River, in his native land. Balak said:

"A people has come out of Egypt; they cover the face of the land and have settled next to me. Now come and put a curse on these people, because they are too powerful for me. Perhaps then I will be able to defeat them and drive them out of the land. For I know that whoever you bless is blessed, and whoever you curse is cursed."

-Numbers 22:5-6

The Moabites were scared because God caused the people of Israel to overcome anyone who opposed them. They thought if they hired a prophet to curse Israel, they could overcome them. Talk about taking warfare to a whole other level.

Balaam said to God, "Balak son of Zippor, king of Moab, sent me this message: 'A people that has come out of Egypt covers the face of the land. Now come and put a curse on them for me. Perhaps then I will be able to fight them and drive them away.'"

-Numbers 22:10-11

I want you to see God's response to His people, who walk honorably unto the Lord.

But God said to Balaam, "Do not go with them. You must not put a curse on those people, because they are blessed." The next morning Balaam got up and said to Balak's officials, "Go back to your own country, for the Lord has refused to let me go with you."

-Numbers 22:12-13

Understand, God would *not* allow this prophet to curse His people. *Why?* Because they were walking in obedience and doing what God called them to do.

Balak did as Balaam said, and the two of them offered a bull and a ram on each altar. Then Balaam said to Balak, "Stay here beside your offering while I go aside. Perhaps the Lord will come to meet with me. Whatever he reveals to me I will tell you." Then he went off to a barren height. God met with him, and Balaam said, "I have prepared seven altars, and on each altar I have offered a bull and a ram." The Lord put a word in Balaam's mouth and said, "Go back to Balak and give him this word." So he went back to him and found him standing beside his offering, with all the Moabite officials. Then Balaam spoke his message: "Balak brought me from Aram, the king of Moab from the eastern mountains. 'Come,' he said, 'curse Jacob for me; come, denounce Israel.' How can I curse those whom God has not cursed? How can I denounce those whom the Lord has not denounced? From the rocky peaks I see them, from the heights I view them.

I see a people who live apart and do not consider themselves one of the nations. Who can count the dust of Jacob or number even a fourth of Israel? Let me die the death of the righteous, and may my final end be like theirs!" Balak said to Balaam, "What have you done to me? I brought you to curse my enemies, but you have done nothing but bless them!" He answered, "Must I not speak what the Lord puts in my mouth?"

-Numbers 23:2-13

The devil cannot curse what God has blessed! I wish the story ended there but it does not. After the people of Israel were blessed and filled with all the wonderful promises of God, they fell into sin and in fact a plague was unleashed in their lives. *How could this be?* Well, Balak learned he could not curse the people of Israel. The only way the protection of God over the people of Israel's lives could be tampered with was if they sinned against the Lord themselves. So, Balaam the wicked prophet counseled the Moabite king to invite Israel to a feast where they worshiped other gods and the Israelite men slept with the Moabite women. This aroused the anger of God and caused God to unleash a plague in which twenty-four thousand people died (*see* Numbers 25:9).

The grace and protection the people of Israel experienced was temporarily lifted because of the sins they committed. *How can a blessed people become a cursed people?* They gave the enemy permission to harass them by what they entertained.

Job said in Job 31:1, "I made a covenant with my eyes not to look lustfully at a young woman." It is safe to say that Job understood the importance of what he let through the doorway of his eyes.

Let's look at another figure in the Bible. King David is referenced as a man after God's own heart (*see* Acts 13:22). King David was a hero of all Jerusalem and a great king in Israel. So great, God allowed his descendent to be the Lord Jesus Christ. Nevertheless, this great king also had a great fall. It happened because he refused to guard the doorway of his eyes.

One evening David got up from his bed and walked around on the roof of the palace. From the roof he saw a woman bathing. The woman was very beautiful, and David sent someone to find out about her. The man said, "She is Bathsheba, the daughter of Eliam and the wife of Uriah the Hittite." Then David sent messengers to get her. She came to him, and he slept with her. (Now she was purifying herself from her monthly uncleanness.) Then she went back home. The woman conceived and sent word to David, saying, "I am pregnant."

-2 Samuel 11:2-5

This is one of the most tragic stories in the Bible. This great king of Israel fell. He fell because instead of turning his eyes from evil, He stared at a woman taking a bath, arousing lustful desire. He longed for her and although he found out she was married, he called her and slept with her anyway.

This act led to great heartache. David had Bathsheba's husband killed and married her to cover his sin (*see* 2 Samuel 11:15, 26-27). God later struck the first child David conceived with Bathsheba, the child became ill and died (*see* 2 Samuel 12:15-18).

Later, Absalom, another one of David's sons conspired against him, and even slept with David's concubines (see 2 Samuel 15:12-14 and 2 Samuel 16:22). *How did all of this chaos erupt?* Because David did not protect the doorway of his eyes. Instead of fleeing from sin, he gazed, lingered, desired, and then touched.

> Flee from sexual immorality. All other sins a person commits are outside the body, but whoever sins sexually, sins against their own body.
>
> -1 Corinthians 6:18

The corruption we feed our eyes will affect our behavior and eventually cause us to stumble. Keep the doorways of your eyes closed. Choose like Job *not* to look at sinful things. Only, let light in and stay away from darkness.

> But if your eye is bad, your whole body will be full of darkness. If therefore the light that is in you is darkness, how great is that darkness!
>
> -Matthew 6:23 NKJV

Prayer of Deliverance:

When you have opened a doorway to the enemy through your eyes, pray this prayer:

Lord, forgive me for setting my eyes on evil things. I understand that through my eyes I can let light and darkness in.

Lord, I let darkness into my eyes by _____ (name the sin and be honest with God).

Lord, I renounce this and break all evil covenants established through my eyes by what I watched.

In the name of Jesus, I command every spirit that has entered my life through the gateway of my eyes to leave now, in the name of Jesus. Amen.

Come quickly in agreement with God. Ask the Lord to fill you with the Holy Spirit. The Holy Spirit will reveal to you things you have set your eyes on that are not good. Get rid of those things so the doorway can remain shut. Listen to the voice of the Holy Spirit as He leads you into victory.

2: Doorway of the Ears

The doorway of the ears can lead the people of God into bondage. What we listen to affects us in many ways.

> Finally, brothers and sisters, whatever is true, whatever is noble, whatever is right, whatever is pure, whatever is lovely, whatever is admirable—if anything is excellent or praiseworthy—think about such things.
>
> -Philippians 4:8

- <u>Demonization: Listening to Ungodly Music</u>

One of the greatest deceptions of our time is found in the music industry, resulting in the pollution of a generation and the bondage of many children and adults. There is a satanic agenda that is *not* hidden and can be plainly seen.

I remember watching an interview with a certain pop star. She attributed her success to selling her soul to Satan. The desire for wealth and fame has caused many to stumble and willfully choose to follow the enemy of our soul. Music is not only melodies and harmonies, but messages. Music is a vehicle to communicate ideas and thoughts. While the tune may be catchy its message can be just as spiritually dangerous as watching a horror movie because of its promotion of violence, homosexuality, pornography, illicit sex, and rape. In fact, I have known of famous rappers who boasted they raped women and children with delight.

When listening to this type of music, we are also picking up the intent of the author, who created the lyrics. When an author is trying to convey a message of hope, we feel it through the music. The same is true when the intended message proclaims violence.

Personally, I remember listening to gangster rap as a kid. It always filled me with this sense of violence and power. It was deceptive, it set me on edge, looking for a fight. I now realize, it filled me with a gangster spirit.

Music has the ability to transmit things spiritually. A great illustration is found in the book of 1 Samuel.

> The Spirit of the Lord had left Saul, and an evil spirit from the Lord was terrifying him. "It's an evil spirit from God that's frightening you," Saul's officials told him. "Your Majesty, let us go and look for someone who is good at playing the harp. He can play for you whenever the evil spirit from God bothers you, and you'll feel better."
>
> "All right," Saul answered. "Find me someone who is good at playing the harp and bring him here."

"A man named Jesse who lives in Bethlehem has a son who can play the harp," one official said. "He's a brave warrior, he's good-looking, he can speak well, and the Lord is with him."

Saul sent a message to Jesse: "Tell your son David to leave your sheep and come here to me."

Jesse loaded a donkey with bread and a goatskin full of wine, then he told David to take the donkey and a young goat to Saul. David went to Saul and started working for him. Saul liked him so much that he put David in charge of carrying his weapons. Not long after this, Saul sent another message to Jesse: "I really like David. Please let him stay with me."

Whenever the evil spirit from God bothered Saul, David would play his harp. Saul would relax and feel better, and the evil spirit would go away.

-1 Samuel 16:14-23 CEV

Notice in this story, an evil spirit would come and torment King Saul. It gained access into Saul's life because of his blatant disregard for God's command. When King Saul was tormented by this spirit, David played the harp and without a word the evil spirit would leave Saul. Notice, the Holy Spirit was present with David while He worshiped God on the harp. In the same way, when someone who is *not* filled with the Holy Spirit sings or plays an instrument the spirit that resides in them is also present, communicated, and flows through their music. We are *not* only being influenced by the words of the music as we listen. We are also influenced by the spirit in the person who is playing the music.

Job 34:3 says, "For the ear tests words as the tongue tastes food." The ears have the ability to take in what they hear as our tongue has the ability to taste food. In other words, through the doorway of the ears you eat the words you hear.

When I was younger, I freestyled and made rap songs. I listened to instrumental music as I slept, hoping it would inspire me to write music. One night, when I was a teenager, about sixteen years old, I fell asleep listening to an instrumental. When I woke up the next morning, a song immediately came to my mind and the words flowed steadily. The only problem was the words that came from my mouth mocked the second coming of Christ. It scared me when I heard myself say what I said. I asked myself, "How can this be? I am a Christian."

Well, the instrumental music I listened to was from a popular rap group of that time. I thought if I listen to the instrumental without the lyrics I could spare myself the foul language and write good music. I did not yet associate the instrumental as dishonoring God. Separating the lyrics from the music did not change the intention of the creator of the song. In turn, I opened a spiritual door by listening to music that did not honor the Lord. Through the doorway of the ears, we let in good or evil, based on what we choose to listen to.

Years later, I worked for a certain company. I was older and much more committed to the Lord. My spiritual life really took a turn, and I had begun seeking God more. God began to use me mightily and I was gradually introduced to the Ministry of Deliverance by the Lord. I met a young man at my job who moved out of his family's home and now lived on his own. He used to go to church but walked away from God. We developed a friendship, and I urged him to go back to church. One day, he confessed to me that he could not sleep at night. He said he felt a dark presence in his room. We prayed together. The Lord impressed my heart to ask him what kind of music he listened to.

I explained to him the importance of *not* listening to any music that does not please God. He asked me to pray for him again. After the prayer, the Lord led me to tell him to get rid of his music and anything else in his house that was not of God. When I saw him the next day, he told me he got rid of his music and some posters in his room, and asked God to forgive him. He slept like a baby. This young man's torment came from what he listened to. He opened a spiritual door to evil by listening to evil. This does not only apply to music but also to listening to false teaching.

- <u>Demonization: Listening to False Teaching</u>

> Now the Spirit expressly says that in latter times some will depart from the faith, giving heed to deceiving spirits and doctrines of demons, speaking lies in hypocrisy, having their own conscience seared with a hot iron,

> -1 Timothy 4:1-2 NKJV

This chapter of the Bible opens with Paul teaching Timothy what the Holy Spirit declared concerning the last days. I want to remind you that the apostles had a unique experience with God. Like the Old Testament prophets, they received direct words from God they recorded, producing the Scriptural account we have today.

What Paul expressed to Timothy is even more relevant to us today, being nearer to the last days. The Spirit of God warned the church that in the last days men will depart from the faith. People will stop following Jesus and choose another path. They will follow deceptive spirits and doctrines of demons.

Literally, this passage says people will be deceived, influenced, and taught by demons.

Just as God has His messengers teach the word of God, Satan has his messengers teach deception and lies. Paul said they, "speak lies in hypocrisy, having their own conscience seared with a hot iron." The conscious is destroyed and cannot speak truth; therefore, it is left only with lies. Most frightening is that these teachers are not only coming from outside the church but also, they are coming from within the church.

> For I have not shunned to declare to you the whole counsel of God. Therefore take heed to yourselves and to all the flock, among which the Holy Spirit has made you overseers, to shepherd the church of God which He purchased with His own blood. For I know this, that after my departure savage wolves will come in among you, not sparing the flock. Also from among yourselves men will rise up, speaking perverse things, to draw away the disciples after themselves. Therefore watch, and remember that for three years I did not cease to warn everyone night and day with tears.
>
> -Acts 20:27-31 NKJV

Paul had such a pastor's heart. His main concern was that the whole counsel of God must be taught to the church. He did *not* cherry-pick what passages of Scriptures to teach and only focus on the content that made people feel good. He taught the entire counsel of the word of God to prepare the congregation. He gave them everything he could, the Scriptures that are pleasant to hear and the ones that are not so pleasant. Nevertheless, all are imperative for godly development.

He charged them to carry out their God-given mandate as overseers of the flock. Paul clearly warned the church that when he leaves savage wolves will come in among them. *Why?* Because their sole intent will be to devour and kill through false teaching, *not sparing the flock,* seeing each church member as a nice, delicious meal.

Paul warned false teachers will also rise from among them, from within the church, who will speak perverse things to draw away disciples after themselves. This means each pastor must watch out for two groups of people:

- ❖ Wolves who are outside the church

- ❖ And wolves who are inside the church, dressed like sheep

Each waiting for an opportunity to draw the congregation away to follow them into false teaching.

Paul emphasized, "for three years I did not cease to warn everyone night and day with tears." This was a serious message. Paul was purposeful and with surety, could give an account for how he watched out for those he oversaw. *At least twice a day, for three years.*

We live in a time when teaching the Bible is no longer highly important to most people. When I was younger, people came to church to hear the word of God. Now, we have entered a new age of deception. People want an experience with God, outside of Biblical principles.

I want to talk to you about some occult practices bleeding over into, what are *thought* to be, esteemed Christian megachurches. Some of their views publicly expressed demonstrate deception infiltrating their world-wide teaching.

I ordered one of their books trying to make sense of what I heard. The title alone was enough to support what I discerned, but I wanted to explore their view in more detail.

It was the most demonically inspired book I have ever read. I was astonished that this book was written by leaders of a church considered to be *Christian* based.

Please pay close attention and be mindful of some of the concepts they falsely shared and I have summarized below:

- Christians should not run from demonic teaching but embrace it because these demonic teachings really come from God and are being misused by those who practice them.

- Support of quantum mysticism, which is considered a New Age belief centered around channeling positive energy through your mind to access benefits of the universe. Somehow the term *god* is intertwined in the topic, but not as Biblically defined, only as a force.

- Encourages Christians to further study and accept New Age thought. Stating it is okay to practice it if you invite Jesus along.

Let's pause for a moment and think. These thoughts were expressed by a well-known pastor, whose church's original worship songs have become a part of many other churches. They have an established school of ministry and believe it is okay for Christians to essentially get into these demonic practices of witchcraft.

Not all experiences come from God. We are to test spirits by the word of God. Here are some things God says in His word:

Heaven and earth will pass away, but My words will by no means pass away.

-Matthew 24:35 NKJV

So shall my word be that goeth forth out of my mouth: it shall not return unto me void, but it shall accomplish that which I please, and it shall prosper in the thing whereto I sent it.

-Isaiah 55:11 KJV

"If there arises among you a prophet or a dreamer of dreams, and he gives you a sign or a wonder, and the sign or the wonder comes to pass, of which he spoke to you, saying, 'Let us go after other gods'—which you have not known—'and let us serve them,' you shall not listen to the words of that prophet or that dreamer of dreams, for the Lord your God is testing you to know whether you love the Lord your God with all your heart and with all your soul. You shall walk after the Lord your God and fear Him, and keep His commandments and obey His voice; you shall serve Him and hold fast to Him. But that prophet or that dreamer of dreams shall be put to death, because he has spoken in order to turn you away from the Lord your God, who brought you out of the land of Egypt and redeemed you from the house of bondage, to entice you from the way in which the Lord your God commanded you to walk. So you shall put away the evil from your midst.["]

-Deuteronomy 13:1-5 NKJV

Notice in this passage the prophetic word came to pass. That was the deception. *Why?* Because the person's word came to pass in order to entice Israel to follow after other gods. I am not against experiences because God uses them to validate His word. The miracles Jesus performed validated his Messianic office. The people heard the words of Jesus but also experienced the power of Him. You cannot separate one from the other. But unchecked experiences and teaching not filtered through the word of God is dangerous and can lure those who listen to *them* to depart from the faith.

We are not to let our experiences have the final say. But we are to test the spirits by the word of God, expose false teaching, and be diligent so it does not get into the church.

> Beloved, do not believe every spirit, but test the spirits, whether they are of God; because many false prophets have gone out into the world.

-1 John 4:1 NKJV

For such *are* false apostles, deceitful workers, transforming themselves into apostles of Christ. And no wonder! For Satan himself transforms himself into an angel of light. Therefore *it is* no great thing if his ministers also transform themselves into ministers of righteousness, whose end will be according to their works.

-2 Corinthians 11:13-15 NKJV

Another false teaching I have researched, centers around a second Pentecost. Biblically, the Day of Pentecost was when the Holy Spirit filled those who were present, and they received the empowerment to speak in new tongues (*see* Acts 2). I do believe this.

Their concept of a second Pentecost, in summary, equates to a new sound coming forth, able to change human DNA into the genetic makeup of God the Father.

Simply stated, when the second Pentecost comes we will change and become like God. Ultimately, operating in His power and ability to do what He did. For example, to speak directly to cancer and it would stop; to speak directly to an ongoing hurricane and it would leave. Their proposed beliefs indicate that these demonstrations of power will happen instantaneously, as the feats of the fictionalized superheroes portrayed in movies.

Many young people are attracted to the church where these astonishing beliefs are being taught as 'Christianity'. They have a world-wide music ministry saturating the atmosphere where this prideful and twisted indoctrination is springing forth from. Other large churches have adopted their music to attract young people. The 'concerts' are used to work people up emotionally. The lyrics are not necessarily bad. Remember the original intent is to access the doorway of the church, *like a wolf in sheep's clothes,* then present *their* teachings of idolatry. Many people are unable to discern the doorway being opened is deceptive and leads to hell and far from the teachings shared by Jesus of the Bible.

Let me ask you a question: *Who in the Bible promised us that if we disobey God we can become like God?*

> Then the serpent said to the woman, "You will not surely die. For God knows that in the day you eat of it your eyes will be opened, and you will be like God, knowing good and evil."
>
> -Genesis 3:4-5 NKJV

The temptation for man to become like God was given to man from the serpent in the beginning. Now, again this teaching, *to become like God,* has bled into today's church through false teaching by false teachers.

If you sat down with these teachers, they would sincerely communicate their beliefs, in an appealing harmless manner, as did the serpent in the Garden of Eden. Remember, a person can be sincere and still go to hell.

Let me tell you about a sincere group of people who went to hell:

> "Not everyone who says to Me, 'Lord, Lord,' shall enter the kingdom of heaven, but he who does the will of My Father in heaven. Many will say to Me in that day, 'Lord, Lord, have we not prophesied in Your name, cast out demons in Your name, and done many wonders in Your name?' And then I will declare to them, 'I never knew you; depart from Me, you who practice lawlessness!'

> "Therefore whoever hears these sayings of Mine, and does them, I will liken him to a wise man who built his house on the rock: and the rain descended, the floods came, and the winds blew and beat on that house; and it did not fall, for it was founded on the rock.

> "But everyone who hears these sayings of Mine, and does not do them, will be like a foolish man who built his house on the sand: and the rain descended, the floods came, and

the winds blew and beat on that house; and it fell. And great was its fall."

And so it was, when Jesus had ended these sayings, that the people were astonished at His teaching, for He taught them as one having authority, and not as the scribes.

-Matthew 7:21-29 NKJV

What did Jesus say? Not everyone who calls Him Lord shall enter the kingdom of heaven. Calling Jesus your Lord and Savior does not mean you will enter heaven.

To reiterate, Jesus said, "Many will say to Me in that day, 'Lord, Lord, have we not prophesied in Your name, cast out demons in Your name, and done many wonders in Your name?'"

Meaning, Christian service or experiencing the supernatural through Christian service does not mean a person is saved. The ability to cast out demons or speak prophetically is not a sign of salvation.

This is a stern warning to those who emphasize experience over obedience to the word of God. Jesus said they will say they did signs and wonders in His name. To which Jesus responded, "And then I will declare to them, 'I never knew you; depart from Me, you who practice lawlessness!'"

Practicing *lawlessness* is living a life disobedient to the word of God. In these verses, the people actually *thought* they were following the Lord because of their religious experiences but they were deceived. Religious experiences do not replace obedience.

Jesus taught His followers the importance of responding to the word of God. When someone hears the word of God, they must do it. Obedience to God's word is the opposite of lawlessness. *Hear the word and do what it says,* "liken him to a wise man who built his house on the rock: and the rain descended, the floods came, and the winds blew and beat on that house; and it did not fall, for it was founded on the rock."

How do we build on the 'rock'? We build on the rock when we are obedient to the word.

In contrast, when someone hears God's word and does not do what it says, "will be like a foolish man who built his house on the sand: and the rain descended, the floods came, and the winds blew and beat on that house; and it fell. And great was its fall."

What is the storm in this passage? I believe it is the day of Judgement when God will judge the living and the dead. Some will go to everlasting life while others to everlasting death. True evidence someone is a follower of God is a life lived in obedience to the word of God. When we genuinely believe something, our behavior aligns with our belief.

What does obedience to the word of God look like? Well, Jesus said, "I am the way, the truth, and the life. No one comes to the Father except through Me" (*see* John 14:6). It's not by works or religious experiences but by the precious blood of Jesus Christ. Our life should reflect salvation through obedience to the word of God.

Listening to false teaching allows our ears to consume lies and demonic deception, resulting in *falling away* from God and opening the door to the occult.

▪ Demonization: Listening to False Voices

One of the main ways the devil tries to infiltrate the life of believers is by pretending to be the person they are infiltrating. Many times, the devil presents temptation through our own thoughts which come to *our* mind in our *own* voice. He implants a thought in our mind and then speaks to us mimicking our voice to get us to think that we are the one thinking and feeling *contrary* things. These are not our thoughts but his thoughts. The devil hopes we will come in agreement with deceptive hijacking thoughts and adopt them as our own. The moment we accept these thoughts as our own, the infiltration begins.

Remember, the devil only had one conversation with Eve. In that one conversation, he convinced her God was lying to her and holding back from her.

> [B]ut of the fruit of the tree which *is* in the midst of the garden, God has said, 'You shall not eat it, nor shall you touch it, lest you die.'" Then the serpent said to the woman, "You will not surely die. For God knows that in the day you eat of it your eyes will be opened, and you will be like God, knowing good and evil." So when the woman saw that the tree *was* good for food, that it *was* pleasant to the eyes, and a tree desirable to make *one* wise, she took of its fruit and ate. She also gave to her husband with her, and he ate. Then the eyes of both of them were opened, and they knew that they *were* naked; and they sewed fig leaves together and made themselves coverings.
>
> -Genesis 3:3-7 NKJV

Notice, Satan caused Eve to doubt *if* God was given her His best. He gave her the entire garden to eat from. The tree in the middle of the garden was off limits. The serpent caused Eve to doubt God's goodness toward her. He convinced her that she could be like God. Satan's biggest deception is to make us think we can be like God. We cannot be like God.

God alone is perfect and wise. He alone can know of evil and *not* let it corrupt Him.

The devil also deceives people by using audible voices that sound like God's voice but are not. Many Christians hear voices that are not their own voices or the voice of God. Those voices are familiar spirits giving misleading advice, causing a person to second guess themselves or instill irrational fears. Fears like, 'you're gonna die', or 'get into a bad accident', or 'something bad is going to happen to you'. Don't allow these voices to go unchallenged by the word of God. These demons try to embed themselves in the mind of people to control the personality of the person. Their goal is to make people think they are crazy and fall into psychosis.

When people listen to these voices long enough and do not challenge them by the word of God, they lose the ability to distinguish between what is their voice versus the devil's voice.

Listening to ungodly music, false teaching, and the whispers of the enemy *and* believing them, result in bondage.

Prayer of Deliverance:

When you have heard ungodly music, false teaching, or the whisper of the enemy and obeyed the deceptive voice, pray this prayer:

Lord, forgive me for coming into agreement with what I heard. Forgive me for not testing what I heard by Your word. Forgive me for allowing myself to be entertained by music that is of a different spirit and not your Holy Spirit. Forgive me for coming into agreement with thoughts, feelings, and emotions that are not from You and Your word.

Today I break all covenants I have made with the enemy through my ears. Lord, I command every evil spirit that came through the doorway of my ears to come out, in Jesus' name. Amen.

If there are specific things the Holy Spirit shows you, confess them and ask the Lord Jesus to deliver you and fill you with His Spirit in this area of your life.

3: Doorway of Generational Curses

When I was a prison chaplain an inmate requested to speak with me in my office. I responded, "Sure, I can speak with you."

He said to me, "Chap, I do not know why I keep going to prison. Every time I get out of prison, I tell myself I am not going back."

The Holy Spirit told me it was a generational curse. Prompted by the Spirit, I asked, "Was your father in prison also?"

He answered, "Yes, he was."

Again, prompted by the Holy Spirit I asked, "Was your grandfather in prison?"

His response was the same, "Yes, he was."

Three generations had succumbed to the spirit of incarceration. The Bible makes clear that the sin of the father can be passed down to the third and fourth generations, if not dealt with (*see* Exodus 34:7).

One of the most tragic stories in the Bible is when King David the warrior of Israel, a man after God's own heart, committed a horrible and wicked sin. David was a man given over to lust. When we first read this story, we *could* think David just kinda fell into sin. But I want you to know that no one just falls into sin. It is often something that has been brewing, marinating, simmering, cultivating, and growing for a long time. Let's go deep into David's life and uncover the root of lust, where it first appeared, and how it affected his children. Please open your Bible to 2 Samuel 11:

> It happened in the spring of the year, at the time when kings go out to *battle*, that David sent Joab and his servants with him, and all Israel; and they destroyed the people of Ammon and besieged Rabbah. But David remained at Jerusalem.

> Then it happened one evening that David arose from his bed and walked on the roof of the king's house. And from the roof he saw a woman bathing, and the woman *was* very beautiful to behold. So David sent and inquired about the woman. And *someone* said, "*Is* this not Bathsheba, the daughter of Eliam, the wife of Uriah the Hittite?" Then David sent messengers, and took her; and she came to him, and he lay with her, for she was cleansed from her impurity; and she returned to her house. And the woman conceived; so she sent and told David, and said, "I *am* with child."

> Then David sent to Joab, *saying*, "Send me Uriah the Hittite." And Joab sent Uriah to

David. When Uriah had come to him, David asked how Joab was doing, and how the people were doing, and how the war prospered. And David said to Uriah, "Go down to your house and wash your feet." So Uriah departed from the king's house, and a gift *of food* from the king followed him. But Uriah slept at the door of the king's house with all the servants of his lord, and did not go down to his house. So when they told David, saying, "Uriah did not go down to his house," David said to Uriah, "Did you not come from a journey? Why did you not go down to your house?"

And Uriah said to David, "The ark and Israel and Judah are dwelling in tents, and my lord Joab and the servants of my lord are encamped in the open fields. Shall I then go to my house to eat and drink, and to lie with my wife? *As* you live, and *as* your soul lives, I will not do this thing."

Then David said to Uriah, "Wait here today also, and tomorrow I will let you depart." So Uriah remained in Jerusalem that day and the next. Now when David called him, he ate and drank before him; and he made him drunk. And at evening he went out to lie on his bed with the servants of his lord, but he did not go down to his house.

In the morning it happened that David wrote a letter to Joab and sent *it* by the hand of Uriah. And he wrote in the letter, saying, "Set Uriah in the forefront of the hottest battle, and retreat from him, that he may be struck down and die." So it was, while Joab besieged the city, that he assigned Uriah to a place where he knew there *were* valiant men. Then the men of the city came out and fought with Joab. And *some* of the people of the servants of David fell; and Uriah the Hittite died also.

Then Joab sent and told David all the things concerning the war, and charged the messenger, saying, "When you have finished telling the matters of the war to the king, if it happens that the king's wrath rises, and he says to you: 'Why did you approach so near to the city when you fought? Did you not know that they would shoot from the wall? Who struck Abimelech the son of Jerubbesheth? Was it not a woman who cast a piece of a millstone on him from the wall, so that he died in Thebez? Why did you go near the wall?'—then you shall say, 'Your servant Uriah the Hittite is dead also.' "

So the messenger went, and came and told David all that Joab had sent by him. And the messenger said to David, "Surely the men prevailed against us and came out to us in the field; then we drove them back as far as the entrance of the gate. The archers shot from the wall at your servants; and *some* of the king's servants are dead, and your servant Uriah the Hittite is dead also."

Then David said to the messenger, "Thus you shall say to Joab: 'Do not let this thing displease you, for the sword devours one as well as another. Strengthen your attack against the city, and overthrow it.' So encourage him."

When the wife of Uriah heard that Uriah her husband was dead, she mourned for her husband. And when her mourning was over, David sent and brought her to his house, and she became his wife and bore him a son. But the thing that David had done displeased the Lord.

-2 Samuel 11 NKJV

David, at the height of victory, the chosen king of Israel, a man after God's own heart, followed the trail of lust, to adultery, then to conspire murder. The accolades of David were not given by man, but by God Himself. The Bible tells us that the previous king of Israel, named Saul, lived a rebellious disobedient life. God removed Saul from his place as told by Samuel the prophet announcing, "The Lord has sought for Himself a man after His own heart," in reference to David.

> But now your kingdom shall not continue. The Lord has sought for Himself a man after His own heart, and the Lord has commanded him *to be* commander over His people, because you have not kept what the Lord commanded you."

> -1 Samuel 13:14 NKJV

This is an important lesson to learn. *While the call of God on your life may be forever, ministry positions are not.* Living in disobedient dishonors God, who removes people from ministry and replaces them. This is a humbling reminder. Serving the Lord is a privilege and not a right. It is His ministry. It is His kingdom. He chooses who gets to be where. Be careful how you serve, so you don't lose your position.

This particular evening, David was in his home, and looked out his window, and saw a beautiful woman bathing. We know this woman was not just uncovered but naked. She was beautiful to behold. When David saw her bathing, he sent for her, and slept with her.

Notice, David did not stop and pray to ask God to help him overcome lust. Nor did David take his desire to his wives. He had several wives and concubines he could have been with.

The marriage bed is the place God has given us to fulfill intimate desires. David did not seek God in prayer. Instead, David took this woman and slept with her.

Out of control areas in our lives breed sin. Sin opens the doorway to other sin. It will never be *just* lust, *just* pornography, *just* lying, or *just* being controlling. These open doors give access to other sins and other spirits.

David went from being a man of lustful spirit to a man operating in a spirit of manipulation and control. He used his powerful position to seduce a married woman.

The spirit of deception took the lead in an attempt to conceal the consequence of David's sin. Bathsheba was pregnant. David tried to trick her husband to go home to sleep with his wife. He called the man home from war, talked with him, and told him to go to his house and wash his feet. All in hopes Uriah would go home, after being deprived of his sexual needs while at war, see his wife, and make love to her. David's scheme did not work.

David escalated his plan and got Uriah drunk thinking now he would surely go home and sleep with his wife. However, Uriah was such a righteous man, he refused to take comfort in his house or wife while the ark of God and the army of Israel were still at war.

> And Uriah said to David, "The ark and Israel and Judah are dwelling in tents, and my lord Joab and the servants of my lord are encamped in the open fields. Shall I then go to my house to eat and drink, and to lie with my wife? *As* you live, and *as* your soul lives, I will not do this thing."
>
> -2 Samuel 11:11 NKJV

When David realized he could not trick Uriah to go home and sleep with his wife to cover up his own adultery, he plotted to have Uriah killed. He wrote a letter to Joab and had Uriah placed in a fierce part of the battle, where he was ultimately killed. The Bible says, "But the thing that David had done displeased the Lord." Notice the progression:

⇒ Lust opened the door for manipulation
⇒ Manipulation opened the door for control
⇒ Control opened the door for abuse of power
⇒ Abuse of power opened the door for murder

I know I'm not the first to point out, "The sin we do not deal with is often multiplied in the lives of our children." This thought is supported over and over in the Scriptures. God shared His respond to David's choices through the prophet Nathan in 2 Samuel 12:

> Then the Lord sent Nathan to David. And he came to him, and said to him: "There were two men in one city, one rich and the other poor. The rich *man* had exceedingly many flocks and herds. But the poor *man* had nothing, except one little ewe lamb which he had bought and nourished; and it grew up together with him and with his children. It ate of his own food and drank from his own cup and lay in his bosom; and it was like a daughter to him. And a traveler came to the rich man, who refused to take from his own flock and from his own herd to prepare one for the wayfaring man who had come to him; but he took the poor man's lamb and prepared it for the man who had come to him."
>
> So David's anger was greatly aroused against the man, and he said to Nathan, "*As* the Lord lives, the man who has done this shall surely die! And he shall restore fourfold for the lamb, because he did this thing and because he had no pity."
>
> Then Nathan said to David, "You *are* the man! Thus says the Lord God of Israel: 'I anointed you king over Israel, and I delivered you from

the hand of Saul. I gave you your master's house and your master's wives into your keeping, and gave you the house of Israel and Judah. And if *that had been* too little, I also would have given you much more! Why have you despised the commandment of the Lord, to do evil in His sight? You have killed Uriah the Hittite with the sword; you have taken his wife *to be* your wife, and have killed him with the sword of the people of Ammon. Now therefore, the sword shall never depart from your house, because you have despised Me, and have taken the wife of Uriah the Hittite to be your wife.' Thus says the Lord: 'Behold, I will raise up adversity against you from your own house; and I will take your wives before your eyes and give *them* to your neighbor, and he shall lie with your wives in the sight of this sun. For you did *it* secretly, but I will do this thing before all Israel, before the sun.' "

So David said to Nathan, "I have sinned against the Lord."

And Nathan said to David, "The Lord also has put away your sin; you shall not die. However, because by this deed you have given great occasion to the enemies of the Lord to blaspheme, the child also *who is* born to you shall surely die." Then Nathan departed to his house.

-2 Samuel 12:1-15 NKJV

God told David, "The sword shall never depart from your house." It is interesting to note the sword even moved into David's home. God did not allow the child who was produced through David and Bathsheba's adulterous relationship to live.

2 Samuel 13 shares that David's son Amnon fell in love with his half-sister Tamar. Instead of asking for her hand in marriage, his cousin helped him devise a plan to sleep with her. Once Amnon got Tamar alone in his room, he manipulated her and raped her. Probably because of his own sins, although angry David did nothing to correct or discipline his son.

This thing ate Absalom up. He was Tamar's full brother because they had the same mother. Absalom held his peace for two whole years and then plotted his vengeance. He planned a party and invited all his brothers. During the party, when Amnon's heart was merry with wine, Absalom's servants killed Amnon as Absalom had commanded (*see* 2 Samuel 13:28-29).

The rest of King David's sons ran for their lives. David received a false report that all his sons were dead and was overcome with mourning. He then found out; it was only Amnon who was dead, and Absalom fled.

Later, 2 Samuel 15 reveals Absalom conspired to steal the hearts of the people, to convince the nation to elect him as king. He aimed to overthrow his father. He took his father's concubines and had sex with them on top of the roof so all of Israel could see (*see* 2 Samuel 16:21-22).

David commanded his servants who were with him at Jerusalem, "Arise, and let us flee, or we shall not escape from Absalom. Make haste to depart, lest he overtake us suddenly and bring disaster upon us, and strike the city with the edge of the sword" (*see* 2 Samuel 15:14).

Over time, a battle transpired in the forest of Ephraim, between David's army and Absalom's army.

> So the men went out into the field against Israel, and the battle was fought in the forest of Ephraim. The men of Israel [who supported Absalom] were defeated there by the men of David, and a great slaughter took place there that day, 20,000 men. For the battle there was spread out over the surface of the entire countryside, and the [hazards of the] forest devoured more men that day than did the sword.
>
> Now Absalom met the servants of David. Absalom was riding on his mule, and the mule went under the thick branches of a massive

tree, and his head was caught in [the thick branches of] the tree; and he was left hanging [in midair] between heaven and earth, while the mule that had been under him kept going.

-2 Samuel 18:6-9 AMP

Absalom was then killed. Joab thrusted three spears through Absalom's heart and ten of Joab's armor bearers surrounded, struck, and killed Absalom (*see* 2 Samuel 18:14-15). This is the same Joab who David ordered to have Uriah killed.

The sin David did not deal with showed up in the lives of his sons:

⇒ Abuse of Power: Amnon forced himself on his sister and raped her.

⇒ Murder: David conspired Uriah's murder. Absalom plotted Amnon's murder. David ordered Joab to have Uriah killed. Joab also participated in the killing of Absalom, David's son.

⇒ Lust: David took Uriah's wife to be his wife to cover up his lustful act with Bathsheba. Absalom slept with his father's concubines to make himself, "odious to his father. Then the hands of all who are with you will be

strengthened [by your boldness and audacity]"
(*see* 2 Samuel 16:21 AMP).

Lust rapidly escalated into much more than
momentary sexual pleasure. Remember what I said in
the beginning. People don't *just* fall into sin.
Oftentimes, it is something that has been cooking for
a long while. Sin had lingered, and not been
adequately dealt with as it should have been. Perhaps,
you have tried to control sin instead of killing it.

> For if you live according to the flesh you will
> die; but if by the Spirit you put to death the
> deeds of the body, you will live.

> -Romans 8:13 NKJV

So, let's look at when David's lust problem began:

> And David took more concubines and wives
> from Jerusalem, after he had come from
> Hebron. Also more sons and daughters were
> born to David.

> -2 Samuel 5:13 NKJV

The custom of the time was for kings to have many
wives. When David took more wives to himself it was
not because he *needed* more wives. David's excessive
marriages to these women was a vehicle for his lust.
Instead of finding satisfaction with the wives he had,
he continued to add more. He did not kill the lust in

his life. He found a culturally accepted way to fulfill it, nonetheless this was not God's design for marriage.

Today, it has become accepted by our culture for people to date with no intention of getting married. *Why?* To fulfill their lust. *How do I know God is not pleased with this?* Deuteronomy 17:14-19 says:

"When you come to the land which the Lord your God is giving you, and possess it and dwell in it, and say, 'I will set a king over me like all the nations that *are* around me,' you shall surely set a king over you whom the Lord your God chooses; *one* from among your brethren you shall set as king over you; you may not set a foreigner over you, who *is* not your brother. But he shall not multiply horses for himself, nor cause the people to return to Egypt to multiply horses, for the Lord has said to you, 'You shall not return that way again.' Neither shall he multiply wives for himself, lest his heart turn away; nor shall he greatly multiply silver and gold for himself.

"Also it shall be, when he sits on the throne of his kingdom, that he shall write for himself a copy of this law in a book, from *the one* before the priests, the Levites. And it shall be with him, and he shall read it all the days of his life, that he may learn to fear the Lord his God and be careful to observe all the words of this law and these statutes,["]

-Deuteronomy 17:14-19 NKJV

Notice the Bible said, "neither shall the king multiply wives for himself." *Why?* So, his heart does not turn away from the Lord. David, instead of dealing with his lust, found a way to deal with the unacceptable.

Because David did not deal with lust, it led to adultery. His adultery led to deception and murder. His son then became a rapist, and his other son became a murderer.

There is no such thing as secret sin. Sin not dealt with affects our homes and our children. I say secret sin because David's lust problem was not known. It was hidden under the *name* of marriage.

When God points out sin in your life don't hide it, don't excuse it, don't ignore it, and don't pretend it will *just* go away. You must kill it. You must not let it live. You must go to war against *that* thing and forbid it to be fed by disobedience.

> For if you live according to the flesh you will die; but if by the Spirit you put to death the deeds of the body, you will live.

-Romans 8:13 NKJV

If your right eye causes you to sin, pluck it out and cast *it* from you; for it is more profitable for you that one of your members perish, than for your whole body to be cast into hell. And if your right hand causes you to sin, cut it off and cast *it* from you; for it is more profitable for you that one of your members perish, than for your whole body to be cast into hell.

-Matthew 5:29-30 NKJV

What did Jesus say? Kill sin. Cut sin off. Don't allow sin to live in you. Don't allow the parasite of sin to feed on you. *Why?* Because it is better to have one eye missing and go to heaven than to have the whole body cast into hell. It is better to have one arm missing than to have the whole body cast into hell.

If you do not kill the sin in your life, it will kill you. If you do not rule over sin, it will devour you.

If you do well, will you not be accepted? And if you do not do well, sin lies at the door. And *its* desire is for you, but you should rule over it."

-Genesis 4:7

The generational sins of lust, adultery, murder, and manipulation, which is a form of witchcraft, were passed down to David's children. The open door to this generational curse was David's private lust problem.

> Therefore submit to God. Resist the devil and he will flee from you. Draw near to God and He will draw near to you. Cleanse *your* hands, *you* sinners; and purify *your* hearts, *you* double-minded.

> -James 4:7-8 NKJV

David is not the only Biblical example we should learn from. Abram, later known as Abraham, lied which invoked a pattern of lying within his family.

> Now there was a famine in the land, and Abram went down to Egypt to dwell there, for the famine *was* severe in the land. And it came to pass, when he was close to entering Egypt, that he said to Sarai his wife, "Indeed I know that you *are* a woman of beautiful countenance. Therefore it will happen, when the Egyptians see you, that they will say, 'This *is* his wife'; and they will kill me, but they will let you live. Please say you *are* my sister, that it may be well with me for your sake, and that I may live because of you."

> So it was, when Abram came into Egypt, that the Egyptians saw the woman, that she *was* very beautiful. The princes of Pharaoh also saw

her and commended her to Pharaoh. And the woman was taken to Pharaoh's house. He treated Abram well for her sake. He had sheep, oxen, male donkeys, male and female servants, female donkeys, and camels.

But the Lord plagued Pharaoh and his house with great plagues because of Sarai, Abram's wife. And Pharaoh called Abram and said, "What *is* this you have done to me? Why did you not tell me that she *was* your wife? Why did you say, 'She *is* my sister'? I might have taken her as my wife. Now therefore, here is your wife; take *her* and go your way." So Pharaoh commanded *his* men concerning him; and they sent him away, with his wife and all that he had.

-Genesis 12:10-20 NKJV

Notice in this story, Abram believed his lie would ensure his safety. Let's look at another passage of Scripture, to emphasize the generational pattern of lying.

So Isaac dwelt in Gerar. And the men of the place asked about his wife. And he said, "She *is* my sister"; for he was afraid to say, "*She is* my wife," *because he thought*, "lest the men of the place kill me for Rebekah, because she *is* beautiful to behold." Now it came to pass, when he had been there a long time, that Abimelech king of the Philistines looked through a window, and saw, and there was Isaac, showing endearment to Rebekah his wife. Then Abimelech called Isaac and said, "Quite obviously she *is* your wife; so how could you say, 'She *is* my sister'?"

Isaac said to him, "Because I said, 'Lest I die on account of her.' "

And Abimelech said, "What *is* this you have done to us? One of the people might soon have lain with your wife, and you would have brought guilt on us." So Abimelech charged all *his* people, saying, "He who touches this man or his wife shall surely be put to death."

-Genesis 26:6-11 NKJV

In comparison, Isaac did the same thing his father did. When he was scared, he lied. He told Abimelech, the king of the land, that his wife was his sister. This pattern of lying and deception did not end with Isaac. It carried on with his two sons, Jacob and Esau.

Now Rebekah was listening when Isaac spoke to Esau his son. And Esau went to the field to hunt game and to bring *it*. So Rebekah spoke to Jacob her son, saying, "Indeed I heard your father speak to Esau your brother, saying,

'Bring me game and make savory food for me, that I may eat it and bless you in the presence of the Lord before my death.' Now therefore, my son, obey my voice according to what I command you. Go now to the flock and bring me from there two choice kids of the goats, and I will make savory food from them for your father, such as he loves. Then you shall take *it* to your father, that he may eat *it*, and that he may bless you before his death."

And Jacob said to Rebekah his mother, "Look, Esau my brother *is* a hairy man, and I *am* a smooth-*skinned* man. Perhaps my father will feel me, and I shall seem to be a deceiver to him; and I shall bring a curse on myself and not a blessing."

But his mother said to him, "*Let* your curse *be* on me, my son; only obey my voice, and go, get *them* for me." And he went and got *them* and brought *them* to his mother, and his mother made savory food, such as his father loved. Then Rebekah took the choice clothes of her elder son Esau, which *were* with her in the house, and put them on Jacob her younger son. And she put the skins of the kids of the goats on his hands and on the smooth part of his neck. Then she gave the savory food and the bread, which she had prepared, into the hand of her son Jacob.

So he went to his father and said, "My father."

And he said, "Here I am. Who *are* you, my son?"

Jacob said to his father, "I *am* Esau your firstborn; I have done just as you told me; please arise, sit and eat of my game, that your soul may bless me."

But Isaac said to his son, "How *is it* that you have found *it* so quickly, my son?"

And he said, "Because the Lord your God brought *it* to me."

Isaac said to Jacob, "Please come near, that I may feel you, my son, whether you *are* really my son Esau or not." So Jacob went near to Isaac his father, and he felt him and said, "The voice *is* Jacob's voice, but the hands *are* the hands of Esau." And he did not recognize him, because his hands were hairy like his brother Esau's hands; so he blessed him.

Then he said, "*Are* you really my son Esau?"

He said, "I *am*."

He said, "Bring *it* near to me, and I will eat of my son's game, so that my soul may bless you." So he brought *it* near to him, and he ate; and he brought him wine, and he drank. Then his father Isaac said to him, "Come near now and kiss me, my son." And he came near and kissed him; and he smelled the smell of his clothing, and blessed him and said:

"Surely, the smell of my son *is* like the smell of a field which the Lord has blessed. Therefore may God give you of the dew of heaven, of the fatness of the earth, and plenty of grain and wine. Let peoples serve you, and nations bow down to you. Be master over your brethren, and let your mother's sons bow down to you. Cursed *be* everyone who curses you, and blessed *be* those who bless you!"

-Genesis 27:5-29 NKJV

Abram lied to Pharaoh about his wife and said she was his sister (*see Genesis* 12:10-20). Abraham (Abram) lied again and said Sarah (Sarai) was his sister in Gerar (*see* Genesis 20). Abraham recounted that he told Sarah, "This is your kindness that you should do for me in every place, wherever we go, say of me, 'He is my brother'" (*see* Genesis 20:13).

We later see that in Genesis 26:6-11, Isaac, Abraham's son, lied to Abimelech about his wife and said she was his sister.

In Genesis 27:5-29, we read, Isaac's son Jacob, Abraham's grandson, lied to his father and told him he was his brother Esau, to steal the blessing entitled to him as the firstborn.

It is evident, each generation's manipulation grew progressively worse. The question we need to answer is this, "How do we break generational curses?"

Let's find the answer in the Bible.

> And I said: "I pray, Lord God of heaven, O great and awesome God, *You* who keep *Your* covenant and mercy with those who love You and observe Your commandments, please let Your ear be attentive and Your eyes open, that You may hear the prayer of Your servant which I pray before You now, day and night, for the children of Israel Your servants, and confess the sins of the children of Israel which we have sinned against You. Both my father's house and I have sinned. We have acted very corruptly against You, and have not kept the commandments, the statutes, nor the ordinances which You commanded Your servant Moses.["]
>
> -Nehemiah 1:5-7 NKJV

Nehemiah prayed a very interesting prayer which we can learn from. The people of Israel sinned against God. The nation sinned and served other gods. So, God allowed them to be overtaken by other nations. The wall of Jerusalem was broken down and the people of Israel were left exposed to enemy attacks. In a sense, it represented that they no longer had God's protection because He allowed an invasion of the country due to their sin. Before God allowed their walls to be rebuilt, Nehemiah did something we need to pay close attention to.

Foremost, Nehemiah recognized there was a sin problem. There was a breach in the wall and a lack of protection because of sin.

Then Nehemiah confessed the sins of the nations and of his father. He acknowledged sin continued without being addressed and eliminated.

After Nehemiah's earnest prayer of repentance, God allowed Nehemiah to rebuild and restore the wall which had been broken down, and left Jerusalem exposed to the enemy.

Why did Nehemiah confess the sins of his parents and then himself? Because Nehemiah understood who God revealed Himself to be.

Now the Lord descended in the cloud and stood with him there, and proclaimed the name of the Lord. And the Lord passed before him and proclaimed, "The Lord, the Lord God, merciful and gracious, longsuffering, and abounding in goodness and truth, keeping mercy for thousands, forgiving iniquity and transgression and sin, by no means clearing *the guilty*, visiting the iniquity of the fathers upon the children and the children's children to the third and the fourth generation."

-Exodus 34:5-7 NKJV

God declared something about Himself we must understand. He declared Himself to be, "The Lord, the Lord God, merciful and gracious, longsuffering, and abounding in goodness and truth, keeping mercy for thousands, forgiving iniquity and transgression and sin," and also the same God, "by no means clearing *the guilty*, visiting the iniquity of the fathers upon the children and the children's children to the third and the fourth generation."

Iniquity is the sin of the heart, for example having a lustful heart.

Transgression is when the sin of the heart becomes an action, when the literal act takes place, for example adultery.

A hateful heart is iniquity, while murder is transgression. Transgression is committing the very act, which flowed from a heart of iniquity.

God revealed, although He is loving; forgiving; full of mercy, goodness, and truth; He will not leave the guilty unpunished but will visit the iniquity of the fathers upon the children and the children's children to the third and the fourth generation.

The walls that were broken down were restored after Nehemiah recognized and acted on this principle to break generational curses. The Holy Spirit led him to pray a prayer of repentance, then provided the strategy, provision, and favor to restore physically what was restored spiritually, through prayer and fasting (see Nehemiah 1:4). Let us apply what God has focused our attention on in this book, *No More Open Doors.*

Recognize There is a Problem

Confess and repent for sin, known or unknown, on behalf of yourself and your parents going back to the third and fourth generation. Revoke access of sin throughout the bloodline. Command that spirit to leave your life, forever.

Submit and Resist

Therefore submit to God. Resist the devil and he will flee from you. Draw near to God and He will draw near to you. Cleanse *your* hands, *you* sinners; and purify *your* hearts, *you* double-minded.

-James 4:7-8 NKJV

Freedom from something does not mean temptation ceases indefinitely. We must submit to the word of God and resist coming out from the place of submission when the devil tries to lure us, in order to maintain our freedom.

Renew Your Mind

And do not be conformed to this world, but be transformed by the renewing of your mind, that you may prove what *is* that good and acceptable and perfect will of God.

-Romans 12:2 NKJV

Every sin has a thinking pattern attached to it. Let's investigate the spirit of rejection. The mindset of someone who battles with rejection is:

I am not enough. I am unloved. Only people's approval of me can give me value.

Personally, I confessed and commanded the spirit of rejection out of my life. Then I went to the Scriptures to change my way of thinking. Every time thoughts of rejection came to my mind; I recited Scriptures affirming my acceptance by God. As I submitted, resisted, and renewed my mind by the word, I was no longer a candidate to house the spirit of rejection. Rejection no longer has a hold on me.

Prayer of Deliverance:

When you recognize a generational curse in your life and you see a dysfunctional pattern shared among your family, pray this prayer:

> Lord, forgive me for _____ (name the sin, pattern, or dysfunction you see in your family and in yourself).
>
> Lord, forgive me and my family going back to the fourth generation.
>
> Pray and say, "Lord, break every legal ground given to the enemy to torment me and my family. I command, in the name of Jesus, for the spirit of _____ to leave now, in Jesus' name.

There may be multiple things God shows you. Do not rush this process. Wait patiently for God to speak to you. As many things as He reveals to you, renounce each of them. Confess them by name and command them to go in Jesus' name. Amen.

As you are praying, you may feel like coughing, vomiting, yelling, and even crying. These things are normal during the deliverance process. God is breaking the hold of the enemy off you and setting you free. Do not fear, God is delivering you. If you need help go to a Bible believing Spirit-filled church and seek help.

4: Doorway of Rape and Trauma

As I write this chapter, I am aware of the sensitivity of this topic. Be cautioned, it may trigger hurt from previous victimization or past experiences. Although that is not my intention, I felt it necessary to disclose before we go on. My goal is to expose how the enemy comes in through wounds.

As someone who has ministered deliverance, I have prayed for people who have experienced violations of the deepest kind. People who have been molested or raped. People who have been demonized *not* because of their own sin but because the devil took advantage of their trauma. Satan will take advantage of despair and lure people into bondage.

The Bible tells the story of Tamar, who was not only raped, but raped by a family member she was assigned to care for.

> In the course of time, Amnon son of David fell in love with Tamar, the beautiful sister of Absalom son of David.

> Amnon became so obsessed with his sister Tamar that he made himself ill. She was a virgin, and it seemed impossible for him to do anything to her.

Now Amnon had an adviser named Jonadab son of Shimeah, David's brother. Jonadab was a very shrewd man. He asked Amnon, "Why do you, the king's son, look so haggard morning after morning? Won't you tell me?"

Amnon said to him, "I'm in love with Tamar, my brother Absalom's sister."

"Go to bed and pretend to be ill," Jonadab said. "When your father comes to see you, say to him, 'I would like my sister Tamar to come and give me something to eat. Let her prepare the food in my sight so I may watch her and then eat it from her hand.'"

So Amnon lay down and pretended to be ill. When the king came to see him, Amnon said to him, "I would like my sister Tamar to come and make some special bread in my sight, so I may eat from her hand."

David sent word to Tamar at the palace: "Go to the house of your brother Amnon and prepare some food for him." So Tamar went to the house of her brother Amnon, who was lying down. She took some dough, kneaded it, made the bread in his sight and baked it. Then she took the pan and served him the bread, but he refused to eat.

"Send everyone out of here," Amnon said. So everyone left him. Then Amnon said to Tamar, "Bring the food here into my bedroom so I may eat from your hand." And Tamar took the bread she had prepared and brought it to her brother Amnon in his bedroom. But when she took it to him to eat, he grabbed her and said, "Come to bed with me, my sister."

"No, my brother!" she said to him. "Don't force me! Such a thing should not be done in Israel! Don't do this wicked thing. What about me? Where could I get rid of my disgrace? And what about you? You would be like one of the wicked fools in Israel. Please speak to the king; he will not keep me from being married to you." But he refused to listen to her, and since he was stronger than she, he raped her.

Then Amnon hated her with intense hatred. In fact, he hated her more than he had loved her. Amnon said to her, "Get up and get out!"

"No!" she said to him. "Sending me away would be a greater wrong than what you have already done to me."

But he refused to listen to her. He called his personal servant and said, "Get this woman out of my sight and bolt the door after her." So his servant put her out and bolted the door after her. She was wearing an ornate robe, for this was the kind of garment the virgin daughters of the king wore. Tamar put ashes on her head and tore the ornate robe she was wearing. She put her hands on her head and went away, weeping aloud as she went.

Her brother Absalom said to her, "Has that Amnon, your brother, been with you? Be quiet for now, my sister; he is your brother. Don't take this thing to heart." And Tamar lived in her brother Absalom's house, a desolate woman.

When King David heard all this, he was furious. And Absalom never said a word to Amnon, either good or bad; he hated Amnon because he had disgraced his sister Tamar.

-2 Samuel 13:1-21

Tamar experienced trauma through rape. She was literally a victim in every sense. She was lured into a trap. She had good intentions. She really thought her brother was sick, and her father sent her to cook and care for him. She had no idea her brother was in love with her nor desired her sexually.

She did not do anything to cause her brother to act inappropriately with her. It was not her dress. She was not being flirtatious. The reason why I mention this is because those who have been victimized by rape or molestation often have shared, they felt like they did something to cause the person who violated them to do the evil act. The root of sin is in the heart of the perpetrator, not the victim.

Tamar fell into Amnon's trap. Many people who were abused have expressed their battle with self-defeating thoughts, such as, "I was so stupid. How did I let myself get into this position." Accompanied by feelings of powerlessness and humiliation. Clearly, in the story we just read, it said Amnon was stronger than her which means to me that she tried to resist him and could not keep him off her.

Many people who have experienced the trauma of rape later verbalized that their sexual identity was stolen. Some began to seek same sex partners because as a young child they experienced sexual pleasure by the same gender, causing them to leave their natural desire for the opposite sex. Sometimes when the perpetrator was the opposite sex, the victims grew to hate the opposite sex and adopted a homosexual lifestyle.

I have also spoken with people who said their violation caused them to become promiscuous. Demonic influence can overly sexualize people to the point where they feel as if they have no control of their sexual desires. Their sexual appetite goes beyond boundaries.

Demonic influence can even cause the spirit of the perpetrator to manifest desires within their victim to commit the same violation that happened to them on others. Working as a prison chaplain, people shared with me that they sexually victimized others in the same way family members, family friends, or others victimized them.

One gentleman I prayed for was violated by his grandfather. His grandfather violated both male and female children. This young man tried what his grandfather did to him on other people and it landed him in prison.

Now, I know this man's victimization does not excuse his violation of others. He knew he deserved to be in prison. Nevertheless, the spirit of rape and molestation was transferred to him. He received deliverance in prison from the demons of rape and molestation.

We do not fully know what Tamar battled with after her trauma nor do I want to add to the text my opinion. But the Bible does say she lived in desolation. In Hebrew, 'desolation'[1] means she lived in ruin, to tremble, which means she lived in fear.

She lived in constant fear and felt as if she was ruined. Many victims of sexual abuse feel stained by the event(s) and rejected. Not all open doors are a result of our own sins. Some are the result of sins done to us.

Below is a list of demons that may need to be cast out as result of trauma:

1. Spirit of fear
2. Spirit of terror
3. Spirit of disassociated reality (when people try to disconnect from the fact of what happened or is happening)
4. Spirit of mourning
5. Spirit of death
6. Spirit of suicide
7. Spirit of lust
8. Spirit of promiscuity
9. Spirit of perversion
10. Spirit of homosexuality
11. Spirit of bisexuality
12. Spirit of powerlessness
13. Spirit of humiliation
14. Spirit of shame
15. Spirit of guilt
16. Spirit of rape
17. Spirit of molestation
18. Abortion

Prayer of Deliverance:

Perhaps you may have experienced such a violation as one spoken of in this chapter. It is not your fault and God wants to set you free from the torment of that victimization. This prayer will be different from others. Pray this prayer:

> Lord, I divorce (name the perpetrator). Lord, break every connection and soul tie to (name the perpetrator). In Jesus' name, I command every part of (name the perpetrator) who has attached himself / herself to me to leave now, in Jesus' name. I command every part of me that is tied to him / her to return to me, in Jesus' name. Amen.

As the Holy Spirit leads you, go back through the list of spirits provided on page 91. The Lord may highlight ones that are affecting you. Command them to leave your life. If you find yourself weeping, don't be alarmed. Often, God will use your tears as a doorway to freedom. God is breaking the shame and disgrace you felt and is setting you free. Be of great courage. God has set you free.

5: Doorway of Demonized Objects

Once I was given some clothes by a friend. When I put the clothes on, I became severely tormented. I prayed and the Lord told me to get rid of the clothes. I gathered everything I was given and threw it away. The torment immediately stopped.

That same night, I went to bed and began to feel tormented again. The Lord gave me a prophetic dream. He took me into my closet and showed me there was one more pair of pants that needed to be thrown away. In the dream, He showed me where the pants were. I woke up from the dream, went to my closet, and there were the pants on a hanger in my closet. I threw them away and confessed and renounced any demons attached to the clothes. Then I had peace.

I pondered the question, *How in the world did this happen to me? Is there any Scriptural evidence of things being infused with supernatural properties?*

Now God worked unusual miracles by the hands of Paul, so that even handkerchiefs or aprons were brought from his body to the sick, and the diseases left them and the evil spirits went out of them.

-Acts 19:11-12 NKJV

These Scriptures give insight into the spiritual realm. God allowed the anointing in Paul's life to be transferred to an inanimate object. In layman's terms, Paul's handkerchief was filled with the Holy Spirit. Since, God's presence can be transferred to a handkerchief, then it is also possible a demonic presence can inhabit an inanimate object.

When I was in high school, a friend of mine told me a strange story. Although I was a Christian, I was not versed in spiritual warfare as I am now. One of his family members gave him a Ouija Board. When he used it, he encountered a demon. It frightened him and he threw it away. The very next day, he found the Ouija Board back in his room. He tried to get rid of it and it would not leave. He was told by the spirit that in order to get rid of it, he would have to give it away to someone else. So, he did.

Looking back and understanding what I understand now, I know demons attach themselves to objects. We are living in a time when witchcraft and New Age practices are on the rise. Many people are putting on crystals, burning sage, displaying figurines of angels from the botanical, and pictures of saints for good luck only to find out they have unknowingly invited demons into their homes.

Remember what I said earlier in this book, the demonic realm gains access through legalities. They operate on the permissions people give them through willful sin, generational sin, and ignorant sin. When a person plays with a Ouija Board, or any other demonic object infused with demonic spirits, unknowingly or knowingly, they give Satan permission to enter their lives by having these objects in their possession.

Therefore, my beloved, flee from idolatry. I speak as to wise men; judge for yourselves what I say. The cup of blessing which we bless, is it not the communion of the blood of Christ? The bread which we break, is it not the communion of the body of Christ? For we, *though* many, are one bread *and* one body; for we all partake of that one bread.

Observe Israel after the flesh: Are not those who eat of the sacrifices partakers of the altar? What am I saying then? That an idol is anything, or what is offered to idols is anything? Rather, that the things which the Gentiles sacrifice they sacrifice to demons and not to God, and I do not want you to have fellowship with demons. You cannot drink the cup of the Lord and the cup of demons; you cannot partake of the Lord's table and of the table of demons. Or do we provoke the Lord to jealousy? Are we stronger than He?

-1 Corinthians 10:14-22 NKJV

I love this passage of Scripture. Paul differentiates between the Lord's table and the table of demons. When we participate in communion, we eat of the Lord's table. It is *not* natural but spiritual. With reverence, we are taking in Christ. The bread and wine are inanimate objects but during communion they symbolize Christ, and we partake of Him.

In the same manner, Paul told the church if they eat food sacrificed to idols, an inanimate object, they are having fellowship with the demons infused in them. These idols are ungodly, and demons are attached to them. If demons are attached to the idols, then demons are attached to the foods offered to the idols.

When I was a prison chaplain, I was shocked to learn how many inmates were in prison for spiritual reasons. I want to tell you a story about a guy named 'Larry'. Larry is not his real name, but this is a true story. He was a Christian who studied occult books to write about the dangers of them. However, these materials, dedicated to demons, were in his home. Larry experienced strange manifestations while reading these materials. He blanked out at times and did not know he blanked out. He shared with me that he committed several robberies and had no idea he did them. He opened a door to demonic spirits through the materials he was researching, and they influenced him. When the police came to Larry's house, he insisted he did not commit the crimes he was accused of. After a careful search of his home, he was caught red-handed. They also had video footage of him committing crimes and he did not remember a single thing. He came to me with this story because he wanted deliverance. We prayed in my office and demons came out of him. During prayers of deliverance, the Holy Spirit guides me to call out specific demons. I was led to call out the names of demons tied to Egyptian gods. After we prayed, I asked Larry to explain to me why the Holy Spirit had me call out Egyptian gods. Larry confessed they were the topics of the books he was reading. This man became demonized by occult material he read. The books were a point of contact for demons.

In fact, the very first demon I cast out in prison came from studying occult material. One day after I led a chapel service, an inmate came to me and asked to talk. I agreed. He said, "I don't know why, but I feel comfortable telling you this. I have spoken to demons, and they are troubling me."

I knew why he felt comfortable speaking to me about this topic. Because my God-given assignment in prison ministry is deliverance. He explained he studied Enochian magic. I invited him into my office and told him if he wanted freedom from these harassing spirits he must repent and renounce his involvement with occult material. We prayed and he experienced deliverance.

Prayer of Deliverance:

If you have demonized objects in your home, you should safely burn them.

> A number who had practiced sorcery brought their scrolls together and burned them publicly. When they calculated the value of the scrolls, the total came to fifty thousand drachmas.

> -Acts 19:19 NIV

We see in the Scripture demonized objects were intentionally removed from the home and burned. If you cannot safely burn them, then throw them away. Pray this prayer:

> Lord, if there are any objects in my home that should not be here, please show me.

As the Lord shows you these things remove them and pray this prayer:

> Lord, I renounce given access to the enemy through _____ (name the object, i.e. book, picture statue, clothing, etc.) to my life.

> Lord, forgive me for having demonized objects in my home. I command every spirit attached to and attracted to these objects to leave me and my home, in Jesus' name. Amen.

<u>Please Note</u>: Crystals, burning sage or incense, displaying statues or pictures of saints, or giving tasks or power to any other inanimate objects does not ward off evil but instead attracts demons into your home. If you have done this, repent and get rid of the demonized objects.

6: Doorway of Unforgiveness

Unforgiveness, I have found, is a sure way a Christian can be demonized. I learned this firsthand during my very first experience leading a time of deliverance. I conducted a lot of research prior to this encounter. I read the Bible and related books, gathered information online, and watched videos about deliverance. One video that stood out to me was in a question-and-answer format. It provided detailed instructions of how to pray for those who are demonized. I found this video shortly after reading the Bible and telling Jesus, "Lord, You casted out demons in the Bible and I want to cast them out as well." Little did I know God took me seriously.

Before I started pastoring my own church, I was on staff at another church. Two young ladies came to talk to me because demonic spirits were tormenting them. They explained to me that since they visited a psychic, they have had terrible nightmares. As I prayed for these young ladies, I set the atmosphere by first asserting my authority in Jesus, then I announced to the demonic spirits, "I am in charge here." During prayer, one of the young ladies began to slither like a snake and a voice came out of her that was not her own. It was a man's voice.

I heard the voice of the Holy Spirit speak in my soul. He said, "Kimani, be bold."

I immediately commanded, "Come out in the name of Jesus."

I continued to pray for her, but the spirit would not come out. Then the Holy Spirit gave me a word of knowledge. These are the words the Holy Spirit spoke to me:

> That spirit's name is *wrath*. It does not want to come out. This woman was abused by her mother when she was a child, and she has refused to forgive her mother.

The other young lady, who came in with the demonized girl, affirmed that this was true. In fact, she said, "Yes, that is exactly what happened to her when she was young."

It was in that moment; the following passage of Scripture in Matthew 18:21-35 came alive to me.

> Then Peter came to Him and said, "Lord, how often shall my brother sin against me, and I forgive him? Up to seven times?"
>
> Jesus said to him, "I do not say to you, up to seven times, but up to seventy times seven. Therefore the kingdom of heaven is like a certain king who wanted to settle accounts with his servants. And when he had begun to settle accounts, one was brought to him who

owed him ten thousand talents. But as he was not able to pay, his master commanded that he be sold, with his wife and children and all that he had, and that payment be made. The servant therefore fell down before him, saying, 'Master, have patience with me, and I will pay you all.' Then the master of that servant was moved with compassion, released him, and forgave him the debt.

"But that servant went out and found one of his fellow servants who owed him a hundred denarii; and he laid hands on him and took *him* by the throat, saying, 'Pay me what you owe!' So his fellow servant fell down at his feet and begged him, saying, 'Have patience with me, and I will pay you all.' And he would not, but went and threw him into prison till he should pay the debt. So when his fellow servants saw what had been done, they were very grieved, and came and told their master all that had been done. Then his master, after he had called him, said to him, 'You wicked servant! I forgave you all that debt because you begged me. Should you not also have had compassion on your fellow servant, just as I had pity on you?' And his master was angry, and delivered him to the torturers until he should pay all that was due to him.

"So My heavenly Father also will do to you if each of you, from his heart, does not forgive his brother his trespasses."

-Matthew 18:21-35 NKJV

What I want to highlight most is in verses thirty-two to thirty-five. These verses are worth reading again.

Then his master, after he had called him, said to him, 'You wicked servant! I forgave you all that debt because you begged me. Should you not also have had compassion on your fellow servant, just as I had pity on you?' And his master was angry, and delivered him to the torturers until he should pay all that was due to him.

"So My heavenly Father also will do to you if each of you, from his heart, does not forgive his brother his trespasses."

-Matthew 18:32-35 NKJV

In this passage, the servant's debt was great, and he could not pay the master back. The master's initial plan to recoup his loan was to sell the servant, his family, and all he had. This large loan of ten thousand talents was now to be paid at the cost of the man, his entire family, and all his possessions. The servant begged the master for more time. The master was compassionate toward him, showed tremendous mercy, and released the man from the debt he owed.

The principle shared in the story is God expects us to forgive others as we have been forgiven.

And be kind to one another, tenderhearted, forgiving one another, even as God in Christ forgave you.

-Ephesians 4:32 NKJV

The servant we read about in Matthew 18 was ungrateful for his master's forgiveness. He found a fellow servant who owed him pennies in comparison to the debt which he was just forgiven. He told him violently, even grabbed him by his throat, "Pay me what you owe!" The servant begged for patience and this ungrateful servant would not give him mercy or forgiveness and threw him in prison.

When the master was told what happened by the other servants, he sent for this ungrateful servant and delivered him to the tortures to have until he paid the debt.

Then Jesus said something very important in Matthew 18:35, "So My heavenly Father also will do to you if each of you, from his heart, does not forgive his brother his trespasses."

As harsh as it sounds, a person with unforgiveness in their heart, is handed over by God to the torturers until forgiveness from the heart is obtained. Many Christians are tormented by the demon of unforgiveness. When a person refuses to forgive someone, this particular demon brings upon the memory of the offense as if it happened yesterday. The person tormented by this demon relives the particular offense, abuse, and hurtful words that were spoken as if the action just happened. This leads to further demonization by means of bitterness, anger, resentment, hatred, and even self-hate.

Throughout my years in ministry, I have found this to be one of the main spirits, probably the number one demonization Christians battle.

Prayer of Deliverance:

The young lady I mentioned in this chapter was bound because she refused to forgive her mother.

To be free from the torment of unforgiveness. We must be willing to forgive those who have harmed us. Forgiveness is an act of the will *not* a feeling. Waiting to feel like forgiving someone indefinitely postpones deliverance from the demonic torturous influence of unforgiveness. Freedom from unforgiveness is found in forgiving.

To be set free from unforgiveness, pray the prayer below, and name the offender and the offense. Naming the offense is crucial for deliverance because you are owning the fact that you were hurt and need God's healing. It breaks the spirit of denial.

> Lord, forgive me for having an unforgiving heart. Lord, I forgive _____ (name the offender) for _____ (name the offense).
>
> Lord, release me from the torment of unforgiveness. In the name of Jesus, I command unforgiveness to leave me. I command anger to leave me. I command bitterness to leave me now, in Jesus' name. Amen.

As you are praying the Holy Spirit will bring other things to your mind that are present. When He does this, command those things to leave. Sometimes God will give you grace and take over the prayer time and begin to remove things out of your life Himself, things you have been unable to identify.

7: Doorway of Fear

Fear is the second most common demon I see come into believers' lives and cause them to miss out on the promises of God. The demon of fear manifests in various fears and phobias. A phobia is defined as:

> A phobia is an uncontrollable, irrational, and lasting fear of a certain object, situation, or activity. This fear can be so overwhelming that a person may go to great lengths to avoid the source of this fear. One response can be a panic attack. This is a sudden, intense fear that lasts for several minutes. It happens when there is no real danger.[1]

The spirit of fear counts on us attaching our beliefs to irrational thoughts, feelings, and emotions. Once we come in agreement with fear through our beliefs in the thoughts pushed upon us by the enemy of our destiny, we open the door to the spirit of fear. In the Bible fear is not described as an emotion. God describes fear as a spirit. It is a demon, not a feeling.

> For God has not given us a spirit of fear, but of power and of love and of a sound mind.

> -2 Timothy 1:7 NKJV

[1]"Phobias." *Johns Hopkins Medicine*, www.hopkinsmedicine.org/health/conditions-and-diseases/phobias#:~:text=A%20phobia%20is%20an%20uncontrollable,can%20be%20a%20panic%20attack. Accessed 6 Mar. 2024.

God does not give us a spirit of fear because *all* fear has to do with irrational thoughts and involves torment (*see* 1 John 4:18). Thoughts *not* based in reality. As Christians, our thoughts must holdfast the word of God as infallible ultimate truth, and *not* our worst imagined thoughts.

When I was a young believer, the enemy would place fear in my mind causing me to believe that something bad was going to happen. I woke up each morning to pray, yet fearful the whole day, expecting for something bad to happen. I was too young in my faith to discern that I was not dealing with a feeling but a demon. This fear trickled into my relationships. I didn't expect good news, instead I anticipated bad happening. Even though I read 2 Timothy 1:7 many times before, I somehow missed God called fear a spirit, *not* a feeling. I did not know how to wage war against it. Building an allegiance with fear, keeps us from the promises and purposes of God. Let's look at this further in 1 Samuel 15:10-25.

> Now the word of the Lord came to Samuel, saying, "I greatly regret that I have set up Saul *as* king, for he has turned back from following Me, and has not performed My command-ments." And it grieved Samuel, and he cried out to the Lord all night. So when Samuel rose early in the morning to meet Saul, it was told Samuel, saying, "Saul went to Carmel, and

indeed, he set up a monument for himself; and he has gone on around, passed by, and gone down to Gilgal." Then Samuel went to Saul, and Saul said to him, "Blessed *are* you of the Lord! I have performed the commandment of the Lord."

But Samuel said, "What then *is* this bleating of the sheep in my ears, and the lowing of the oxen which I hear?"

And Saul said, "They have brought them from the Amalekites; for the people spared the best of the sheep and the oxen, to sacrifice to the Lord your God; and the rest we have utterly destroyed."

Then Samuel said to Saul, "Be quiet! And I will tell you what the Lord said to me last night."

And he said to him, "Speak on."

So Samuel said, "When you *were* little in your own eyes, *were* you not head of the tribes of Israel? And did not the Lord anoint you king over Israel? Now the Lord sent you on a mission, and said, 'Go, and utterly destroy the sinners, the Amalekites, and fight against them until they are consumed.' Why then did you not obey the voice of the Lord? Why did you swoop down on the spoil, and do evil in the sight of the Lord?"

And Saul said to Samuel, "But I have obeyed the voice of the Lord, and gone on the mission on which the Lord sent me, and brought back Agag king of Amalek; I have utterly destroyed the Amalekites. But the people took of the plunder, sheep and oxen, the best of the things which should have been utterly destroyed, to sacrifice to the Lord your God in Gilgal."

So Samuel said: "Has the Lord *as great* delight in burnt offerings and sacrifices, as in obeying the voice of the Lord? Behold, to obey is better than sacrifice, *and* to heed than the fat of rams. For rebellion *is as* the sin of witchcraft, and stubbornness *is as* iniquity and idolatry. Because you have rejected the word of the Lord, He also has rejected you from *being* king."

Then Saul said to Samuel, "I have sinned, for I have transgressed the commandment of the Lord and your words, because I feared the people and obeyed their voice. Now therefore, please pardon my sin, and return with me, that I may worship the Lord."

-1 Samuel 15:10-25 NKJV

Saul was demonized by the fear of men. He was afraid of disappointing the very people he was called to lead. The problem was that he feared the people more than He feared God. He wanted to please man rather than God. He was a man pleaser and the root of this need to make people happy was the fear of men. He feared the rejection of men and did not want to be in opposition to those he was leading. This irrational fear of, *If I don't please them, I'll lose them,* in turn cost Saul the kingdom. King Saul's fear of men cost him the right to rule over them. God stripped him of the kingdom and gave it to David, a man after His own heart.

My father taught me an acronym for fear when I was growing up, *False Expectations Appearing Real.* Fear causes us to believe in outcomes that are not true to God's character and word. Saul actually thought obeying his people would bring a greater blessing than obeying God. He lost the truth. God called Saul to lead the people; *not* follow them. Leaders sometimes have to disappoint people as they follow God. Saul was influenced by the spirit of fear. God rewards faithfulness, *not* disobedience.

The spirit fear caused King Saul to believe the people and their needs were greater than God. The spirit of fear caused King Saul to believe if he obeyed the people, he would not lose his influence over them. Fear over inflates false thoughts and makes us believe the worst will come upon us, as if God has no control. The spirit of fear is a liar.

Believe, God made it clear in His word, He has given us the *spirit* of a sound mind.

> For God has not given us a spirit of fear, but of power and of love and of a sound mind.
>
> -2 Timothy 1:7 NKJV

God has already given us the spirit of a sound mind to bring contrary thoughts under the subjection and control of the Holy Spirit. A sound mind thinks, and problem solves. It is aligned with the Scriptures. A sound mind is rooted in truth.

God has *not* given us irrational minds nor has God given us irrational thoughts. Irrational thoughts, *not* rooted in God's word, discredit the character of God. When influenced by the spirit of fear, we assume God will allow us to be consumed by the worst thing we can imagine or as people say, "My worst fear is ____." God is greater than our fears and will often use even our greatest disappointment for our good and His glory. Be confident, it always works out for a believer for the good.

> And we know that all things work together for good to those who love God, to those who are the called according to *His* purpose.
>
> -Romans 8:28 NKJV

While the spirit of fear capitalizes on many entry points, its primary entry point is disbelief in the promises of God, as it pertains to the children of God. Let's study Numbers 13:30-33 and Numbers 14:1-10.

> Then Caleb quieted the people before Moses, and said, "Let us go up at once and take possession, for we are well able to overcome it."
>
> But the men who had gone up with him said, "We are not able to go up against the people, for they *are* stronger than we." And they gave the children of Israel a bad report of the land which they had spied out, saying, "The land through which we have gone as spies *is* a land that devours its inhabitants, and all the people whom we saw in it *are* men of *great* stature. There we saw the giants (the descendants of Anak came from the giants); and we were like grasshoppers in our own sight, and so we were in their sight."
>
> -Numbers 13:30-33 NKJV

So all the congregation lifted up their voices and cried, and the people wept that night. And all the children of Israel complained against Moses and Aaron, and the whole congregation said to them, "If only we had died in the land of Egypt! Or if only we had died in this wilderness! Why has the Lord brought us to this land to fall by the sword, that our wives and children should become victims? Would it not be better for us to return to Egypt?" So they said to one another, "Let us select a leader and return to Egypt."

Then Moses and Aaron fell on their faces before all the assembly of the congregation of the children of Israel.

But Joshua the son of Nun and Caleb the son of Jephunneh, *who were* among those who had spied out the land, tore their clothes; and they spoke to all the congregation of the children of Israel, saying: "The land we passed through to spy out is an exceedingly good land. If the Lord delights in us, then He will bring us into this land and give it to us, 'a land which flows with milk and honey.' Only do not rebel against the Lord, nor fear the people of the land, for they *are* our bread; their protection has departed from them, and the Lord is with us. Do not fear them."

And all the congregation said to stone them with stones. Now the glory of the Lord appeared in the tabernacle of meeting before all the children of Israel.

-Numbers 14:1-10 NKJV

The people God sent to take a look at the promised land verified it was exceedingly fruitful and filled with evidence of all the blessings God promised. However, when they saw the people who lived there and how tall they were, they allowed themselves to be filled with fear (*see* Numbers 13:27-28 and Numbers 14:7). They became so afraid that they wept and rejected Moses as their leader. Joshua and Caleb tried to remind the children of Israel of God's promise to give them the land and the people who lived there into their hands.

Joshua and Caleb tried to redirect their minds away from the irrational thought that God would set them up for failure and cause them to lose the very battle He promised they would win. Nevertheless, the children of Israel decided to believe the spirit of fear over the truth of God's word. Being filled with fear and not faith, they even said to stone Joshua and Caleb with stones. The influence of the spirit of fear resulted in a great majority of the children of Israel dying in the wilderness and missing out on the promised land and the blessing that awaited them.

And the Lord spoke to Moses and Aaron, saying, "How long *shall I bear with* this evil congregation who complain against Me? I have heard the complaints which the children of Israel make against Me. Say to them, 'As I live,' says the Lord, 'just as you have spoken in My hearing, so I will do to you: The carcasses of you who have complained against Me shall fall in this wilderness, all of you who were numbered, according to your entire number, from twenty years old and above. Except for Caleb the son of Jephunneh and Joshua the son of Nun, you shall by no means enter the land which I swore I would make you dwell in. But your little ones, whom you said would be victims, I will bring in, and they shall know the land which you have despised. But *as for* you, your carcasses shall fall in this wilderness. And your sons shall be shepherds in the wilderness forty years, and bear the brunt of your infidelity, until your carcasses are consumed in the wilderness. According to the number of the days in which you spied out the land, forty days, for each day you shall bear your guilt one year, *namely* forty years, and you shall know My rejection. I the Lord have spoken this. I will surely do so to all this evil congregation who are gathered together against Me. In this wilderness they shall be consumed, and there they shall die.' "

-Numbers 14:26-35 NKJV

This mass hysteria of unbelief was brought through the spirit of fear, the irrational thought that God would *not* be true to His word, that He had *not* given them power to defeat the enemy, and that God was a liar. We know this thinking is false, but the people of Israel believed the lying spirit of fear. Their disbelief in God's truth cost them their prepared entrance into the full promises of God.

The spirit of fear and disbelief partner to destroy God's people. We must, as children of God, challenge every thought, feeling, and emotion in comparison to the word of God and rebuke and cast out the spirit of fear. We must *not* let the lying spirit of fear twist our perception. Let the word of God be your sight and understanding.

Prayer of Deliverance:

This prayer is going to take some introspection. Take some time to identify any fear gripping your life. Then pray and ask God, "What is the root of this fear?" Wait in prayer until the Lord reveals the response. Then pray this prayer:

> Lord, forgive me for agreeing with the spirit of fear and believing that _____ (name the false things you have believed about God, yourself, and what God showed you).

> Lord, I reject and renounce the spirit of fear and I command fear to leave my body and mind now, in Jesus' name. Amen.

As you are praying this prayer, do not be surprised if you feel fearful. This is an intimidation tactic of the enemy to get you to stop praying. Continue to pray as the Lord leads you until the spirit of fear is lifted from you.

8: Doorway of Rejection

Rejection is another spirit that enters into the lives of people. The main entrance point I have seen is through a wound coming from a parent. A child may feel unaccepted by their parent(s) because they are absent; divorced; living separately; or disconnected as a result of overworking, sickness, or a lack of prioritized time with their children because of their own stressors. Instead of feeling love, acceptance, and being wanted by their parent(s), the spirit of rejection influences the person to believe no one loves them nor wants them around.

This spirit is known to cause people to sabotage their relationships. *Why?* This spirit makes people think other people feel as negatively about them as they feel about themselves. People who are demonized by the spirit of rejection enter every relationship guarded and prepared for a fight. They are waiting for the bottom to drop out in every relationship. They communicate in a defensive manner, or they are overly committed in relationships out of fear of being rejected, suffocating those they are in relationships with by their extreme neediness. They tend to seek constant love and affirmation from those around them, often placing undue pressure on people they seek to have in their life.

Rejection and self-rejection work hand in hand to make people feel like they are not enough and not worth being loved. It is a very dangerous spirit and can lead to murderous intentions. This is why I tell parents, "Never-ever say you have a favorite child or make your children feel less than their siblings." Let's look at a Biblical example of this.

> Now Jacob dwelt in the land where his father was a stranger, in the land of Canaan. This is the history of Jacob.
>
> Joseph, *being* seventeen years old, was feeding the flock with his brothers. And the lad *was* with the sons of Bilhah and the sons of Zilpah, his father's wives; and Joseph brought a bad report of them to his father.
>
> Now Israel loved Joseph more than all his children, because he *was* the son of his old age. Also he made him a tunic of *many* colors. But when his brothers saw that their father loved him more than all his brothers, they hated him and could not speak peaceably to him.
>
> Now Joseph had a dream, and he told *it* to his brothers; and they hated him even more. So he said to them, "Please hear this dream which I have dreamed: There we were, binding sheaves in the field. Then behold, my sheaf arose and also stood upright; and indeed your

sheaves stood all around and bowed down to my sheaf."

And his brothers said to him, "Shall you indeed reign over us? Or shall you indeed have dominion over us?" So they hated him even more for his dreams and for his words.

Then he dreamed still another dream and told it to his brothers, and said, "Look, I have dreamed another dream. And this time, the sun, the moon, and the eleven stars bowed down to me."

So he told *it* to his father and his brothers; and his father rebuked him and said to him, "What *is* this dream that you have dreamed? Shall your mother and I and your brothers indeed come to bow down to the earth before you?" And his brothers envied him, but his father kept the matter in mind.

-Genesis 37:1-11 NKJV

See in this story, how the spirit of rejection entered the lives of Jacob's sons. The Bible said, "Now Israel loved Joseph more than all his children, because he *was* the son of his old age." Joseph received special treatment as the *favorite* child. In fact, Jacob gave him a coat of many colors which was as a physical reminder to all his brothers, Joseph was loved more than them.

Naming a favorite child automatically disqualifies every other child and places them in the category of *not the favorite*. We see rejection in its purest form in this story. Joseph's brothers must have felt like they could never measure up to Joseph and be loved as he was loved by their father. The Bible explicitly said, "they hated him [Joseph] even more for his dreams and for his words." This generated anger, resentment, hatred, and later led to attempted murder.

> Then his brothers went to feed their father's flock in Shechem. And Israel said to Joseph, "Are not your brothers feeding *the flock* in Shechem? Come, I will send you to them."
>
> So he said to him, "Here I am."
>
> Then he said to him, "Please go and see if it is well with your brothers and well with the flocks, and bring back word to me." So he sent him out of the Valley of Hebron, and he went to Shechem.
>
> Now a certain man found him, and there he was, wandering in the field. And the man asked him, saying, "What are you seeking?"

So he said, "I am seeking my brothers. Please tell me where they are feeding *their flocks*."

And the man said, "They have departed from here, for I heard them say, 'Let us go to Dothan.'" So Joseph went after his brothers and found them in Dothan.

Now when they saw him afar off, even before he came near them, they conspired against him to kill him. Then they said to one another, "Look, this dreamer is coming! Come therefore, let us now kill him and cast him into some pit; and we shall say, 'Some wild beast has devoured him.' We shall see what will become of his dreams!"

-Genesis 37:12-20 NKJV

Joseph's brothers hated him because he was their dad's favorite child which meant they were not. They felt rejected by their dad. To add fuel to the fire, Joseph was given dreams that he would rule over his family. It is possible they even felt rejected by God.

God has given us earthly fathers to be physical representations of God's love for His people. When a child does not get the security of love from their father, they may believe God has or will also withdraw His love from them, in the same way. This can cause them to believe the lie that even God hates and rejects them. Joseph dreamed of being the leader of his family. His elevation would not have been seen as a threat to his brothers if they received the same fatherly love and affirmation Joseph received. They viewed Joseph as an enemy because of the rejection they felt.

Rejection eventually leads to the fear of men because rejection influences people to feel like the measure of acceptance by man equates to their greatness. Someone demonized by the fear of rejection looks for their value in man instead of finding their value in God. Proverbs 29:25 NKJV says, "The fear of man brings a snare, but whoever trusts in the Lord shall be safe."

Any time we fear men it brings a snare into our lives. The spirit of rejection irrationally determines that a person should fear man and come under the subjection of the views and opinions of man, so they are not rejected. On the contrary, when acceptance comes from God, and we trust in Him, we are kept safe.

The spirit of rejection influences people to believe other people have power over them and end up living their lives trying to please people rather than God because of the fear of being rejected and unloved. People then become masters and gods over people.

Thus says the Lord: "Cursed is the man who trusts in man and makes flesh his strength, whose heart departs from the Lord. For he shall be like a shrub in the desert, and shall not see when good comes, but shall inhabit the parched places in the wilderness, *in* a salt land which is not inhabited.

"Blessed *is the* man who trusts in the Lord, and whose hope is the Lord. For he shall be like a tree planted by the waters, which spreads out its roots by the river, and will not fear when heat comes; but its leaf will be green, and will not be anxious in the year of drought, nor will cease from yielding fruit."

-Jeremiah 17:5-8 NKJV

God is the source. Man and earthly provision are resources. There is a curse on the life of anyone who puts their trust in man, who sees man as the source of their acceptance, or as the source of anything. They will end up dry like a shrub in the desert and unfruitful, living in parched places, places absent from water and life.

A person under the influence of the spirit of rejection often has an empty life because they are trying to drink from a resource that cannot satisfy them. People's approval of you will never satisfy you. The more it is sought after, the emptier one will feel.

Why? Because people can approve of you one day, then disapprove of you the next day. That is too much power to give to another human being.

Read Jeremiah 17:7-8 out loud. It is a promise from God. Seek God. Know you are approved by God. Accept His approval and trust Him as your source.

> "Blessed *is the* man who trusts in the Lord, and whose hope is the Lord. For he shall be like a tree planted by the waters, which spreads out its roots by the river, and will not fear when heat comes; but its leaf will be green, and will not be anxious in the year of drought, nor will cease from yielding fruit."
>
> -Jeremiah 17:7-8 NKJV

Those who trust in God are planted by the waters. Their life is not dry but full. They are fruitful, they live without fear, they are not full of anxiety, and they are blessed. Trusting in God as our source of acceptance allows us to be fully satisfied in all areas of our lives.

Rejection and self-rejection are spirits that have been known to escalate to murder, even mass shootings and suicide, often stemming from bullying and rejection.

Thoughts and ideas like, "No one loves me" (rejection), or, "No one wants me around" (rejection), or, "I am not good enough" (self-rejection) have resulted in cutting and suicide. When dealing with the spirit of rejection, cast these other spirits out as well.

Prayer of Deliverance:

Pray this prayer of deliverance to free yourself from the spirit of rejection:

> Lord, forgive me for believing the lie that I am rejected, and no one loves me. Your word says in Romans 15:7, "Accept one another, then, just as Christ accepted you, in order to bring praise to God."
>
> Today I come in agreement with Your word. I am accepted by You. Only Your acceptance matters.
>
> Lord, today I reject the spirit of rejection. I renounce my submission to its lie. I command the spirit of rejection to leave me now, in Jesus' name. I command the spirit of self-rejection to leave me now, in Jesus' name. I command suicide and death to leave me now, in Jesus' name, I pray. Amen.

As you pray, let the Holy Spirit lead you. Continue to pray as the Holy Spirit prompts you. The Lord will fight for you as You seek Him.

9: Doorway of Witchcraft

Witchcraft is forbidden in the Scriptures and the punishment for practicing witchcraft in Biblical times was death. Below are some things the Bible says about witchcraft:

"You shall not permit a sorceress to live."

-Exodus 22:18 NKJV

'Give no regard to mediums and familiar spirits; do not seek after them, to be defiled by them: I *am* the Lord your God.'

-Leviticus 19:31 NKJV

'And the person who turns to mediums and familiar spirits, to prostitute himself with them, I will set My face against that person and cut him off from his people.'

-Leviticus 20:6 NKJV

As we can see by these Scriptures God does not tolerate Christians practicing witchcraft. I started this chapter with these verses to ensure we understand the severity of opening the door to witchcraft.

God sets His face against those who speak to spirits and contact the dead, who are really demons in disguise. The Lord does not tolerate it and the consequences are grave and dangerous.

While I served as a prison chaplain, a gentleman came to me after chapel and wanted to talk to me about a family situation he was going through. As I listened to his story, the Holy Spirit told me the man was not in prison for the crime they said he committed but because of witchcraft.

I stopped the man in mid-sentence as he was telling his story and I said to him, "As I was sitting here listening to you, the Lord spoke and told me that you are not in prison because of the crime they said you committed. You are in prison because of witchcraft. Do you practice witchcraft?"

He answered, "When I started my business, I paid a man money to cast a spell over my business to make it grow."

I responded, "Sir, you opened the door to demons when you did that. To get freedom, you must fully surrender to Jesus and renounce witchcraft."

He agreed and we prayed together. The Lord showed me flowers on the floor as I prayed for him. I told the man, "The Lord showed me flowers on the floor as I prayed. What does that mean?"

"The man I paid to cast the spell over my business told me to buy certain flowers and arrange them on the floor," he informed me.

My response was, "You must renounce every ritual you committed."

We prayed and the spirit of witchcraft was broken off of him. He was released from prison shortly after our prayer.

Witchcraft promises the practitioner control over life circumstances and people. But demons are behind the veil of witchcraft. Demons have one purpose and that is the total utter destruction of humanity. Jesus said:

> ["]The thief comes only in order to steal and kill and destroy. I came that they may have and enjoy life, and have it in abundance [to the full, till it overflows]."
>
> -John 10:10 AMP

Witchcraft offers partnership with human beings. Remember, demons need to influence people to do things for them. The deception of witchcraft is that it will give people an advantage, but the truth is people are taken advantage of through demonization.

The spirit of witchcraft hides its intent to kill people. This demonization interferes with and aims to destroy all relationships. It is seductive and deceptive. It wants to keep people in total spiritual blindness and bondage. Its ultimate goal is for people to die without Jesus Christ and go to hell.

People who practice witchcraft always feel like they're in control of the spirits they communicate with. However, the reality is the demons are in control of them. Each ritual a person commits gives the demons more control over their life. The person thinks they are gaining more power, but they are giving more control of their lives over to the demons.

The demons cleverly convince people they have power and control but rather they are giving up more and more of their freewill to the demons. Demons torment people who practice witchcraft. People are then influenced to do another spell or another ritual to appease the demons. This is a clever way for the demons to get people to open more doors to be further demonized. These torments are strategically used by the demons to give access to more demons, making the person worse.

We are living in a time when witchcraft has invaded our society in many subtle and bold ways. There is a rise of New Age, ancestral worship, energy crystals, Ouija Boards, and trends to burn sage and oils. These practices promise to balance our energy and cleanse our lives of negativity. These are all lies so Satan can gain the entry point he needs into our lives.

Once Satan gets people to open the doorway of their lives, through these false means of help, he will be able to continue his deception and destroy their lives.

Remember, the man I told you about on page 132, who ended up in prison because he meddled with witchcraft.

One of the things I was shocked about as a prison chaplain was how many inmates made pacts with demons through witchcraft for protection. Many of them confessed to me they made pacts with water spirits so they would not get caught selling drugs. Other inmates made pacts with demons so their drugs would sell better. There is one thing all these inmates have in common, they all ended up in prison. The demons that promised protection and wealth were nowhere to be found behind bars. These spirits cunningly convinced their victims there was a source outside of God. When I explained to the inmates these were not good spirits but evil spirits many of them surrendered their lives to Jesus and renounced their pacts with Satan.

I have witnessed the weeping of joy as people are finally set free from demonic bondage. I have seen the name of Jesus expel every demon. Jesus is still the same God as He was on earth, healing the sick, raising the dead, and casting out demons.

Prayer of Deliverance:

If you have opened the door to witchcraft in your life, please pray this prayer for freedom:

Lord, please forgive me and/or my family for opening the door to witchcraft.

Lord, I renounce every agreement made with demons through _____ (name the practice or things you did).

Lord, today I break covenant with every altar speaking in the spiritual realm declaring my allegiance to demons.

Lord, in the name of Jesus, I divorce myself from the gods of my fathers' households. I declare, in Jesus' name, that You alone are God and I serve You only.

In the name of Jesus, I command every spirit that has entered my life through _____ (name the practice or things you did) to leave me now, in Jesus' name. Amen.

10: Doorway of Tattoos

Early in my Christian walk, I took a neutral stance about tattoos. I did not see them as evil or good. I grew up in a very conservative home, it was something our household just didn't do. However, my view changed when an inmate came to me and asked for prayer because he suffered from a sexual addiction.

As I led him through a series of prayers, the Lord also brought to my attention that there were tattoos of a particular animal on his body. I asked him, "Do you have a tattoo of a snake on your body?"

"Yes," he replied, "I got a tattoo from a man who went to jail for attempted murder."

He was in jail for the same crime. Then the Lord showed me another tattoo on the man's body. It appeared to be some sort of mask. I asked him if he had this particular image on his body.

Again, he confirmed, "Yes, I got that tattoo from a man who had anger issues and now I also suffer from anger issues."

When the man allowed the tattoo artist to cut him and mark him, it created a blood covenant between the artist and the inmate. This allowed for the transferring of spirits between them.

When I researched tattoos, I found out they stem from pagan occult practices. Now, they are more modernized in the west for fashion, or viewed as a symbol of rebellion, or to assert individuality. Nevertheless, the truth is tattoos originated from the occult and are not kingdom transferable.

So, what is a tattoo?

> TATTOO — a permanent mark or design fixed upon the body by a process of pricking the skin and inserting an indelible color under the skin. The moral and ceremonial laws of Leviticus declare, "You shall not make any cuttings in your flesh for the dead, nor tattoo any marks upon you" (Lev. 19:28). Any kind of self-laceration or marking of the body was prohibited among the Hebrew people. Such cuttings were associated with pagan cults that tattooed their followers while they mourned the dead.[1]

Although in our western world we try to repurpose occult practices, the demonic realm is not confused as to what practices belong to them. In fact, they are very happy to know that most Christians are too lazy to research the subject and pray to find out if something should be adopted into their life or not. Not *all* practices are kingdom transferable.

[1]Ronald F. Youngblood, F. F. Bruce, and R. K. Harrison, Thomas Nelson Publishers, eds., Nelson's New Illustrated Bible Dictionary (Nashville, TN: Thomas Nelson, Inc., 1995).

The rise of New Age practices has crept into the church including yoga, crystals, and reiki energy healing. Many Christians are ignorantly inviting demons into their lives without giving a single thought to where these practices are coming from and why they are so popular. I have learned as a minister who deals in deliverance to question everything. I have seen too many Christians end up in spiritual bondage because they lacked the insight to do research.

> My people are destroyed for lack of knowledge; because you have rejected knowledge, I reject you from acting as a priest for me. And since you have forgotten the law of your God, I will also forget your children.
>
> -Hosea 4:6 NKJV

The spiritual realm is real, and demons count on our ignorance to gain a point of entry into our lives.

Prayer of Deliverance:

When I prayed for the inmate with the tattoos, he began to manifest several demonic spirits and in the great name of Jesus, he was set free.

I used this prayer to lead him through repentance for marking his body with tattoos. You can pray this prayer for freedom, as well:

> Lord, forgive me for marking my body with a tattoo. Lord, I command every spirit that entered my body through _____ (name each tattoo on your body) to leave me now, in Jesus' name.

> Lord, break every blood covenant I made between me and the tattoo artist. In the name of Jesus, I command every spirit that transferred from the tattoo artist to me to leave me now, in Jesus' name.

> Lord, today I shut the door between me and the tattoo artist and proclaim through Your blood I am washed, cleansed, and forgiven, in Jesus' name. Amen.

11: Doorway of Freedom

As you read this book, perhaps the Lord pointed something new out to you. Perhaps, you sense that what you have been battling with is not natural but spiritual and you are ready for healing, breakthrough, and freedom.

How can demonized people be set free? Recognizing there is a problem is the first step to your freedom. I want you to understand that deliverance is the children's bread. It is a right that belongs to every child of God. In fact, the Bible speaks of Jesus in Galatians 5:1, "It is for freedom that Christ has set us free. Stand firm, then, and do not let yourselves be burdened again by a yoke of slavery."

Jesus came to set you free. It was His, and is His, purpose to give you complete and utter freedom. He delights in giving us freedom. At least one third of Jesus' ministry was deliverance. Everyone who came to Him bound was set free.

When evening came, many who were demon-possessed were brought to him, and he drove out the spirits with a word and healed all the sick. This was to fulfill what was spoken through the prophet Isaiah: "He took up our infirmities and bore our diseases."

-Matthew 8:16-17

[A]nd Jesus healed many who had various diseases. He also drove out many demons, but he would not let the demons speak because they knew who he was.

-Mark 1:34

When Jesus saw that a crowd was running to the scene, he rebuked the impure spirit. "You deaf and mute spirit," he said, "I command you, come out of him and never enter him again."

The spirit shrieked, convulsed him violently and came out. The boy looked so much like a corpse that many said, "He's dead." But Jesus took him by the hand and lifted him to his feet, and he stood up.

After Jesus had gone indoors, his disciples asked him privately, "Why couldn't we drive it out?"

He replied, "This kind can come out only by prayer."

-Mark 9:25–29

Jesus did not reject those who were bound when they came to Him. He set them free. He is aware of how long our struggles have lasted and what our struggles are. Struggles with things such as pornography, anger, sexual dreams, or other intrusions of the enemy. He is aware of the constant bombardment of wicked thoughts that assault us. He understands the personal torment many of us have endured desiring and learning to live a godly life but being sucked back into the same sin we said we would never go back to.

Jesus has come today to set you free. If you desire to be set free, then pray the Prayer of Deliverance below. During this prayer you may manifest a demonic spirit. You may feel dizzy, nauseated, or start coughing and throwing up. Do not be afraid. Stand in the authority of Jesus Christ and command that spirit to leave your body. It is important that you do not stop yourself or else you may hold the spirit in.

Prayer of Deliverance:

Please pray this prayer:

> God, please forgive me and my family for opening the door to the enemy by _____.

> I renounce giving access to Satan when I did _____. I ask that You break every legal ground I have given over to the enemy in this area of my life.

> In the name of Jesus, I command every spirit that came into my body and mind through _____, to leave now, in Jesus' name. Amen.

If you need further deliverance or want to share your testimony, please reach out to God's Kingdom Church Florida located in Kissimmee, Florida, USA. You do not need to be a member of our church to receive prayer, you just need to be desperate for Jesus.

Give us a call at (407) 799-0391.

Scan to visit us on Facebook and view our service archives:

About the Author

With a heart dedicated to serving God and nurturing souls, Kimani Smith is the Lead Pastor of God's Kingdom Church Florida, USA. As a seasoned minister, he has committed his life to guiding individuals toward spiritual freedom and transformation through the power of Jesus Christ in the ministry of deliverance.

Kimani brings a wealth of experience to his pastoral role, having served in various capacities within the church community. He has served as a devoted Children's Pastor, fostering the spiritual growth and development of young hearts with love and compassion. Additionally, he has taken on the responsibilities of a Missions Pastor, demonstrating a deep commitment to spreading the gospel and serving those in need, both locally and globally.

As an Associate Pastor, Kimani has played a pivotal role in providing guidance, support, and leadership within the church congregation. His dedication to ministry, coupled with his passion for delivering souls from bondage, has inspired countless individuals to experience the transformative love of Jesus Christ.

Driven by a desire to see lives changed and souls saved, Kimani continues to lead God's Kingdom Church Florida, USA alongside with unwavering faith, compassion, and a steadfast commitment to spreading the gospel message of hope, redemption, and deliverance.

Kimani resides in Florida with his wife of twenty years and their four children.

Get Connected with Pastor Kimani Smith:

@PastorKimaniSmith

www.ingramcontent.com/pod-product-compliance
Lightning Source LLC
Chambersburg PA
CBHW071407120626
46546CB00002B/846